A Guide to Writing
KANJI & KANA

Book 1

A Self-Study Workbook for Learning Japanese Characters

Wolfgang Hadamitzky & Mark Spahn

TUTTLE PUBLISHING
Boston • Rutland, Vermont • Tokyo

Published by Tuttle Publishing, an imprint of Periplus Editions (HK) Ltd. with editorial offices at 153 Milk Street, Boston, Massachusetts 02109 and 130 Joo Seng Road, #06-01/03, Singapore 368357.

LCC Card No. 91-65055
ISBN 0-8048-3392-3

Printed in Singapore

Distributed by:

Japan
Tuttle Publishing
Yaekari Building, 3rd Floor
5-4-12 Osaki, Shinagawa-ku
Tokyo 141-0032
Tel: (03) 5437 0171
Fax: (03) 5437 0755
Email: tuttle-sales@gol.com

North America, Latin America & Europe
Tuttle Publishing
364 Innovation Drive
North Clarendon, VT 05759-9436
Tel: (802) 773 8930
Fax: (802) 773 6993
Email: info@tuttlepublishing.com
www.tuttlepublishing.com

Asia Pacific
Berkeley Books Pte. Ltd.
130 Joo Seng Road #06-01/03
Singapore 368357
Tel: (65) 6280 1330
Fax: (65) 6280 6290
Email: inquiries@periplus.com.sg

10 09 08 07 06 05 04
20 19 18 17 16 15

CONTENTS

INTRODUCTION

The purpose of *A Guide to Writing Kanji and Kana* is to help students of Japanese master writing the two *kana* syllabaries (46 hiragana and 46 katakana) and the 1,945 basic characters (Jōyō Kanji) officially recommended for daily use.

With so many characters, it is important that you study them systematically, in a carefully thought-out progression. Most textbooks for learning Japanese, however, do not offer an introduction to Japanese script based on sound didactic principles. *A Guide to Writing Kanji and Kana* answers the need for a step-by-step presentation of characters by following the system developed in the book *Kanji & Kana* [1]. Also, up to three basic graphical elements (graphemes) indicating its meaning and/or pronunciation are listed for each kanji. Furthermore, the characters are taught not in isolation but as parts of important compounds that use only characters that have been introduced earlier.

Characters are presented in brush, pen, and printed forms. Each character in pen form is printed in light gray for you to trace over. These gray lines will guide your hand the first time you try writing a new character and will help you quickly develop a feel for the proper proportions.

When practicing writing the characters, don't forget that they should be written to fit into squares, either real or imaginary, of exactly the same size. *A Guide to Writing Kanji and Kana* has convenient, pre-printed squares: large and normal size for all kana and the first 778 kanji, and normal size for kanji 779–1,945.

The best way to begin learning the Japanese writing system is to start with one of the two syllabaries, either hiragana or katakana. This is because:

1. The number of characters is limited to 46 characters per syllabary.

2. The forms of the characters are simple (there are one to four strokes per kana).

3. Each character has only one pronunciation (except for two characters that have two readings).

4. The kana syllabaries represent the entire phonology of the Japanese language, which means that any text can be written entirely in kana and without using any kanji at all.

---

[1] Hadamitzky, Wolfgang and Mark Spahn: *Kanji & Kana: A Handbook and Dictionary of the Japanese Writing System,* Charles E. Tuttle Company, Rutland, VT and Tokyo, 1981.

It is difficult to say which syllabary should be learned first. If you learn katakana first, even as a beginner you will be able to write many words, especially loanwords from English, that you already know. Hiragana, however, is by far the more widely used syllabary. We recommend the following learning sequence as the quickest way to master hiragana or katakana; for best results, we suggest using, if available, the computer program *SUNRISE Script*[2] to help you learn correct pronunciation.

1. Divide either syllabary into **several small units**. Concentrate on only a few kana at each session. Begin, for instance, with the first five vowels of hiragana.

2. Practice the **pronunciation** of each kana, first while looking at the transcription and later without looking. This will help you link the sound of each kana to its visual image.

3. Memorize the **order of the syllables** (*a-i-u-e-o, ka-ki-ku-ke-ko*) by reading them aloud.

4. Memorize the **shape** of each kana and compare it to that of other kana; take notice of similarities and peculiarities.

5. Memorize the **order** in which the strokes are written and the **direction** in which each stroke is written.

6. **Practice writing** each kana, first writing on the three gray pen forms in the large squares. Practice each kana until you can write it with the correct stroke order, stroke direction, and proportions without looking at the model.

7. Read aloud and **write all the words** that are given as examples for each character. Using *SUNRISE Script*, you can browse through the kana you've learned, manually or automatically, in a given order or at random, at various speeds, and with or without the audio function.

8. After finishing all the characters of either the hiragana or katakana syllabary, **review** them to check your grasp of forms and sounds.

9. **Repeat** the above steps for each unit.

10. **Review regularly**.

When memorizing kanji, use the same method as the one recommended above for the syllabaries. For kanji, look at the **basic graphical elements** (graphemes) the entry character is made up of; you will soon notice that all kanji are constructed from relatively few basic elements. These elements often indicate the meaning and/or pronunciation of the kanji. Instead of following the order of kanji presented in this book, you can choose any order you like. You might, for example, select the order in which kanji are introduced in the textbook you're using in class. The disadvantage to this, however, is that the words and compounds will then contain characters that you have not yet learned.

The kanji are fully indexed by *on-kun* readings. The *Index* in Book 1 lists all kanji contained in that volume. The *General Index* at the end of Book 2 lists all kanji contained in both volumes, grouping together kanji that share the same reading and a common graphical element.

---

[2] Hadamitzky, Wolfgang and Mark Spahn: *SUNRISE Script: Electronic Learning and Reference System for Kanji*, JAPAN Media, Berlin, 1989. (With this computer program you can both hear and read the pronunciation of the characters.)

EXPLANATION OF THE CHARACTER ENTRIES

Hiragana/Katakana

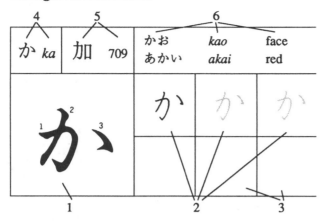

1. The kana character in brush form, with numbers showing stroke order positioned at the beginning of each stroke.

2. Squares with the kana character in pen form, printed in light gray, and serving as a practice template to trace over.

3. Empty squares in which to write first the kana character and then the example words.

4. The kana character in printed form, with pronunciation in roman letters.

5. Kanji from which the kana character is derived, with the sequential number of that kanji.

6. Up to four common words, with romanization and meanings. These words contain only kana that have already been introduced.

Kanji

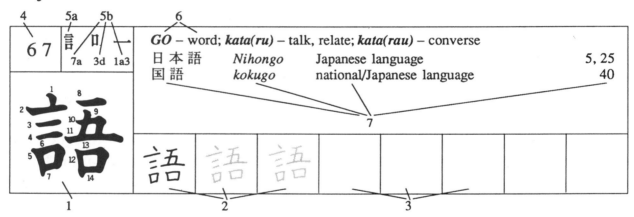

1. The kanji in brush form, with numbers showing stroke order positioned at the beginning of each stroke.

2. Three squares with the kanji in pen form, printed in light gray and serving as a practice template to trace over.

3. Empty squares in which to write the entry kanji and compounds.

4. Number of the kanji in these manuals.

5. a. Radical with its number-and-letter "descriptor", under which the kanji is listed in the *Japanese Character Dictionary* [3].

   b. Up to three graphemes (basic elements) with their number-and-letter "descriptor", under which the kanji can be retrieved in *SUNRISE Script* (see footnote 2).

   A numeral from 2 to 4 added to the descriptor indicates how many times that radical or grapheme is contained in the kanji. If the radical is not a grapheme, it is put in parentheses.

6. *On* readings, in capital italics; *kun* readings, in lowercase italics; readings that are infrequent or used only in special cases, in brackets; *okurigana* (part of a word that is written in kana), in parentheses; English meanings. All officially recognized readings of the kanji are listed.

7. Compounds, with romanization, meanings, and cross-reference numbers to the main entries for other kanji in the compound.

---

[3] Spahn, Mark and Wolfgang Hadamitzky: *Japanese Character Dictionary: With Compound Lookup via Any Kanji*, Nichigai Associates, Tokyo, 1989.

ah

あ	*a*	安	105	ああ	*ā*	ah, oh

あ あ あ あ あ あ あ あ
あ あ あ あ あ あ
あ あ あ あ あ あ あ あ あ あ
あ あ あ あ あ あ あ あ あ あ
あ あ あ あ あ あ あ あ あ あ
あ あ あ あ あ あ あ あ あ あ あ

meet

あ い

い	*i*	以	46	いい	*ii*	good, alright	あい	*ai*	love, affection

い い い い い い い い
い い い い い い い い
い い い あい いい い い い い い
い い い い い い い い
い い い い い い い
い

う	u	宇 990	あう		au		meet		いう	iu		say

う

	う	う	う	う	う	う	う	う
	う	う	う	う	う	う	う	う
う	う	う	う	う	う	う	う	う
う								

う	う	う						

get

え	e	衣 677	え		e		picture, painting	ええ	ē		yes, yeah, uh-huh
			うえ		ue		top, area above	いいえ	iie		no

え

	え	え	え	え	え	え	え
	え	え	え				

え	え	え						

お	o	於	–	あおい	*aoi*	blue, green		おおい	*ōi*	lots of, many

お　お　お　お　お　お　お　お
お　お

お　お　お

か	ka	加	709	かお	*kao*	face		かう	*kau*	buy, purchase
				あかい	*akai*	red		えいが	*eiga*	movie

か　か　か　か　か　か　か　か
か　か　か　か　か　か　か　か

か

か　か　か

が　が　か

き	*ki*	幾	877	あき おおきい	*aki* *ōkii*	autumn big, large	えき かぎ	*eki* *kagi*	(train) station key

き　き　き　き　き　き　き

き　き　き
ぎ　ぎ　ぎ

いく　かく　きく　か

く	*ku*	久	1210	いく かく	*iku* *kaku*	go write	きく かぐ	*kiku* *kagu*	hear; ask furniture

く　く　く　く　く　く

く　く　く
ぐ　ぐ　ぐ

け ke	計 340	いけ	ike	pond		けいき	keiki	times, business

けけけけけけけけ

| け | け け | | | | | | | |
| げ | げ げ | | | | | | | |

こゑ

こ ko	己 370	ここ ごご	koko gogo	here, this place afternoon	こえ えいご	koe eigo	voice English (language)

ここここここここ

| こ | こ こ | | | | | | | |
| ご | ご ご | | | | | | | |

さ *sa*	左	75	さあ さけ	*sā* *sake*	well now, alright saké	あさ けいざい	*asa* *keizai*	morning economy

	さ	さ	さ	さ	さ	さ	さ	さ
	さ	さ	さ	さ	さ	ざ	さ	さ

さ

さ	さ	さ											
ざ	ざ	ざ											

し *shi*	之	–	あし おいしい	*ashi* *oishii*	leg, foot tasty, tastes good	いし あじ	*ishi* *aji*	stone taste, savor

	し	し	し	し	し		

し

し	し	し											
じ	じ	じ											

す	su	寸	1894	すし いす	*sushi* *isu*	sushi chair	あす かず	*asu* *kazu*	tomorrow number

せ	se	世	252	あせ かぜ	*ase* *kaze*	sweat, perspiration wind, breeze	せいじ なぜ	*seiji* *naze*	politics why

そ *so*	曽 –	そう	*sō*	so, like that	そこ	*soko*	there
		うそ	*uso*	lie, falsehood	かぞく	*kazoku*	family

そ (stroke order 1, 2)

そ そ そ

ぞ ぞ ぞ

た *ta*	太 629	たかい	*takai*	high; expensive	した	*shita*	bottom, area below
		かた	*kata*	person (polite)	ただしい	*tadashii*	correct

た (stroke order 1, 2, 3, 4)

た た た

だ だ だ

ち chi	知	214	ちいさい いち	*chiisai* *ichi*	little, small one	ちかい うち	*chikai* *uchi*	near home, residence

ち ち ち ち ち ち ち

ち ち ち

ち　ち　ち

ぢ　ぢ　ぢ

つ tsu	川	33	つぎ いくつ	*tsugi* *ikutsu*	the next how many	つかう がっこう	*tsukau* *gakkō*	use school

つ つ つ つ つ

つ　つ　つ

づ　づ　づ

て	te	天	141	て きって	te kitte	hand (postage) stamp		ちかてつ です	chikatetsu desu	subway be

て　　て　て　て　て　て　て

て　て

て　て　て

で　て　て

と	to	止	477	とおい せいと	tōi seito	far pupil, student		とし いちど	toshi ichido	year; city one time, once

と　　と　と　と　と

と　と　と

ど　ど　ど

な na	奈	-	ななつ nanatsu seven なか naka the inside		なつ natsu summer おなじ onaji the same	

な　な　な　な　な　な　な　な

な な な

に ni	仁 1619	にし nishi west にど nidō twice, two times	にく niku meat なに nani what

に　に　に　に　に　に　に
に　に

に に に

ぬ *nu*	奴 1933	ぬぐ しぬ	*nugu* *shinu*	take/peel off die		いぬ きぬ	*inu* *kinu*	dog silk	
ぬ		ぬ	ぬ	ぬ	ぬ	ぬ	ぬ	ぬ	ぬ
		ぬ	ぬ	ぬ	ぬ	ぬ			
ぬ ぬ ぬ									

ね *ne*	祢 –	ねこ おかね	*neko* *okane*	cat money	ねがい あね	*negai* *ane*	a request elder sister
ね		ね	ね	ね	ね	ね	ね
		ね	ね	ね	ね		
ね ね ね							

の no	乃	–	ので この	*node* *kono*	because, since this	のど たのしい	*nodo* *tanoshii*	throat merry, pleasant

| | の | の | の | の | の | | | |

の の の

は ha/ wa	波	666	はは (は) にばい	*haha (wa)* *nibai*	mother (wa = particle) double, twice as much	はい しっぱい	*hai* *shippai*	yes failure, flop

| は | は | は | は | | | | |

ば ば ば

ぱ ぱ ぱ

ひ *hi*	比	798	ひと	*hito*	person, man		ひがし	*higashi*	east
			くび	*kubi*	neck		いっぴき	*ippiki*	one (animal)

ひ	ひ	ひ	ひ	ひ					

び	び	び							
ぴ	ぴ	ぴ							

ふ *fu*	不	94	ふたつ	*futatsu*	two		ふね	*fune*	ship
			どうぶつ	*dōbutsu*	animal		きっぷ	*kippu*	ticket

ふ	ふ	ふ	ふ	ふ	ふ	ふ	ふ		

ぶ	ぶ	ぶ							
ぷ	ぷ	ぷ							

へ he/e	部 86	へた	heta	unskillfulness	どこへ	doko e	where to
		かべ	kabe	wall	ぺらぺら	perapera	(speak) fluently

へ		ヘ	ヘ	ヘ						
べ	べ	べ								
ぺ	ぺ	ぺ								

ほ ho	保 489	ほか	hoka	other	ほね	hone	bone
		ぼうし	bōshi	hat	ぽかぽか	pokapoka	repeatedly

ほ		ほ	ほ	ほ	ほ					
ぼ	ぼ	ぼ								
ぽ	ぽ	ぽ								

ま *ma*	末	305	まつ しま	*matsu* *shima*	wait island		なまえ いま	*namae* *ima*	name now	

ま ま ま ま

ま ま ま

み *mi*	美	401	みみ うみ	*mimi* *umi*	ear sea, ocean		みせ みなみ	*mise* *minami*	shop, store south	

み み み み み み み

み み み

| む *mu* | 武 1031 | むっつ | *muttsu* | six | むずかしい | *muzukashii* | difficult |
| | | よむ | *yomu* | read | さむい | *samui* | cold |

む む む む

む む む

| め *me* | 女 102 | めいし | *meishi* | name card | あめ | *ame* | rain |
| | | だめ | *dame* | useless, vain | いつつめ | *itsutsume* | the fifth |

め め め め

め め め

も mo	毛 287	もの もじ	*mono* *moji*	thing, object character, letter	もう もっと	*mō* *motto*	already more		
も		も	も	も					
も	も	も							

や ya	也 -	やすい やま	*yasui* *yama*	cheap, inexpensive mountain	やさしい ひゃく	*yasashii* *hyaku*	easy, simple hundred		
や	や	や	や	や	や	や	や		
や	や	や							

ゆ *yu*	由 363	ゆき	*yuki*	snow	ゆうめい	*yūmei*	famous
		ふゆ	*fuyu*	winter	きゅう	*kyū*	nine

ゆ ゆ ゆ ゆ ゆ ゆ ゆ ゆ ゆ

ゆ ゆ ゆ

よ *yo*	与 539	よい	*yoi*	good, alright	よむ	*yomu*	read
		よっつ	*yottsu*	four	きょう	*kyō*	today

よ よ よ

よ よ よ

ら *ra*	良	321	から ひらがな	*kara* *hiragana*	from; because hiragana	いくら さようなら	*ikura* *sayōnara*	how much goodbye

ら ら ら ら ら ら ら ら ら

ら ら ら

り *ri*	利	329	かなり まつり	*kanari* *matsuri*	quite, rather festival	あります りょこう	*arimasu* *ryokō*	be (present) trip, travel

り り り り り り

り り り

る *ru*	留 761	くる よる	*kuru* *yoru*	come (at) night, evening	ある ふるい	*aru* *furui*	be old

る　る　る　る　る　る　る　る　る
る　る　る　る　る　る　る　る

る　る　る

れ *re*	礼 620	れい かれ	*rei* *kare*	example he	これ きれい	*kore* *kirei*	this pretty; clean

れ　れ　れ　れ　れ　れ　れ
れ　れ　れ　れ　れ

れ　れ　れ

ろ *ro*	呂	-	ろく	*roku*	six		いろ	*iro*	color
			しろい	*shiroi*	white		ところ	*tokoro*	place

ろ　　ろ　ろ　ろ　ろ　ろ　ろ　ろ

ろ　ろ　ろ

わ *wa*	和	124	わたし	*watashi*	I		わかる	*wakaru*	understand
			わるい	*warui*	bad, evil		にわ には	*niwa ni wa*	in the garden

わ　　わ　わ　わ　わ　わ　わ　わ

わ　わ　わ

を	o	遠	446	おちゃ を のむ　*ocha o nomu*　drink (green) tea しお を かう　*shio o kau*　buy salt

を ををを を ろ をを
をををを

を を を

ん	n	尤	–	なん　　　　*nan*　　what おんな　　*onna*　　woman	よん　　　　*yon*　　four かんぱい　*Kanpai!*　To your health!

ん ん ん ん ん ん

ん ん ん

| ア | a | 阿 | – | アー | *aa* | ah, oh |

| ア | ア | ア | | | | | | |

| ア | ア | ア | | | | | | | | | | | |

| イ | i | 伊 | – | イー | *ii* | good, alright | アイ | *ai* | love, affection |

| イ | イ | イ | | | | | | |

| イ | イ | イ | | | | | | | | | | | |

ウ	u	宇	990	アウ	*au*	meet		イウ	*iu*	say

ウ ウ ウ

ウ ウ ウ

エ	e	江	821	エ	*e*	picture, painting		エー	*ee*	yes, yeah, uh-huh
				ウエ	*ue*	top, area above		イーエ	*iie*	no

エ エ エ

エ エ エ

					アオイ	*aoi*	blue, green	オーイ	*ooi*	lots of, many

オ *o* 於 –

オ オ オ

オ	オ	オ										

カ *ka* 加 709

カー *kā* car

カ カ カ

カ	カ	カ											

ガ ガ ガ

| キ *ki* | 幾 877 | キー   *kī*   key |

| ク *ku* | 久 1210 | アーク   *āku*   (electric) arc |

ケ - コ

ケ *ke*	介 453	ケーキ *kēki* cake			オーケー *ōkē* O.K., okay		

ケ | ケ | ケ | ケ |

ケ
ゲ | ゲ | ゲ

コ *ko*	已 370	コア *koa* core			ゴア *goa* Goa		

コ | コ | コ | コ |

コ | コ | コ
ゴ | ゴ | ゴ

サ *sa*	散 767	サー	*sā*	sir

サ	サ	サ	サ					

| サ | サ | サ | | | | | | | | | | | |
| ザ | ザ | ザ | | | | | | | | | | | |

シ *shi*	之 –	シガー	*shigā*	cigar	アジア	*ajia*	Asia

シ	シ	シ						

| シ | シ | シ | | | | | | | | | | | |
| ジ | ジ | ジ | | | | | | | | | | | |

ス *su*	須	–	スキー コース	*sukī* *kōsu*	skiing, skis course	ガス スイス	*gasu* *Suisu*	gas Switzerland		
ス	ス	ス	ス							
ス	ス	ス								
ズ	ズ	ズ								

セ *se*	世	252	セクシー	*sekushī*	sexy	ガーゼ	*gāze*	gauze		
セ	セ	セ	セ							
セ	セ	セ								
ゼ	ゼ	ゼ								

ソ *so*	曽	-	ソース	*sōsu*	sauce		ソーセージ	*sōsēji*	sausage
			ソれん	*Soren*	Soviet Union				

ソ

ソ	ソ	ソ						
ゾ	ゾ	ゾ						

タ *ta*	多	229	タクシー	*takushī*	taxi		ウエーター	*uētā*	waiter
			ギター	*gitā*	guitar		えいがスター	*eiga sutā*	movie star

夕

夕	夕	夕						
ダ	ダ	ダ						

チ chi	千	15	チーズ	*chīzu*	cheese		チェス	*chesu*	chess	

チ	チ	チ	チ						

チ	チ	チ											
ヂ	ヂ	ヂ											

ツ tsu	川	33	スーツケース	*sūtsukēsu*	suitcase		クッキー	*kukkī*	cookie	
			サッカー	*sakkā*	soccer		チェック	*chekku*	check	

ツ	ツ	ツ							

ツ	ツ	ツ											
ヅ	ヅ	ヅ											

| テ | te | 天 | 141 | データ | *dēta* | data | | ディスク | *disuku* | disk |
| | | | | シーディー | *shīdī* | CD (compact disk) | | | | |

テ　テ　ラ　ラ

テ　ラ　ラ

デ　ブ　ブ

| ト | to | 止 | 477 | テスト | *tesuto* | test | | テキスト | *tekisuto* | text |
| | | | | スカート | *sukāto* | skirt | | ドット | *dotto* | dot |

ト　ト　ト

ト　ト　ト

ド　ド　ド

ナ na	奈	-	ナチ (ス)	*nachi(su)*	the Nazis		カナダ	*Kanada*	Canada

ナ　ナ　ナ　ナ

ナ　ナ　ナ

ニ ni	仁	1619	ニーズ	*nīzu*	needs		テニス	*tenisu*	tennis

二　二　二　二

二　二　二

ヌ *nu*	奴 1933	ヌード	*nūdo*	nude	カヌー	*kanū*	canoe

ヌ

ヌ	ヌ	ヌ					

ヌ	ヌ	ヌ										

ネ *ne*	袮 –	ネクタイ ネガ	*nekutai* *nega*	necktie (photographic) negative	ゼネスト	*zenesuto*	general strike

ネ

ネ	ネ	ネ					

ネ	ネ	ネ										

ノ no	乃	-	ノー	*nō*	no		ノート	*nōto*	notebook
ノ		ノ	ノ	ノ					

ノ	ノ	ノ											

ハ ha	八	10	バス	*basu*	bus		バナナ	*banana*	banana
			スーパー	*sūpā*	supermarket		デパート	*depāto*	department store
ハ		ハ	ハ	ハ					

バ	バ	バ											
パ	パ	パ											

ヒ _hi_	比	798	コーヒー	_kōhī_	coffee		ビデオ	_bideo_	video
			サービス	_sābisu_	service		コピー	_kopī_	copy

ヒ	ヒ	ヒ	ヒ						
ビ	ビ	ビ							
ピ	ピ	ピ							

フ _fu_	不	94	ナイフ	_naifu_	knife		ストーブ	_sutōbu_	stove
			コップ	_koppu_	(drinking) glass		フォーク	_fōku_	fork

フ	フ	フ	フ						
ブ	ブ	ブ							
プ	プ	プ							

へ *he*	部	86	ベッド	*beddo*	bed		データーベース	*dētābēsu*	database
			ページ	*pēji*	page				

へ

| ベ | ベ | ベ |
| ペ | ペ | ペ |

ホ *ho*	保	489	ホステス	*hosutesu*	hostess		ボーナス	*bōnasu*	bonus
			ポスト	*posuto*	post(box)		スポーツ	*supōtsu*	sports

ホ

| ボ | ボ | ボ |
| ポ | ポ | ポ |

マ *ma*	末	305	ママ テーマ	*mama* *tēma*	mama theme	パーマ マーケット	*pāma* *māketto*	permanent (wave) market
マ			マ	マ	マ			

ミ *mi*	三	4	ミニカー マスコミ	*minikā* *masukomi*	minicar mass communication	ミス ゼミ	*misu* *zemi*	mistake; Miss seminar
ミ			ミ	ミ	ミ			

ム mu	牟	–	ゲーム ハム	*gēmu* *hamu*	game ham		ブーム けしゴム	*būmu* *keshigomu*	boom eraser

ム ム ム

ム ム ム

メ me	女	102	メーデー メキシコ	*mēdē* *Mekishiko*	May Day Mexiko		メッセージ メッカ	*messēji* *Mekka*	message Mecca

メ メ メ

メ メ メ

モ *mo*	毛	287	モーター メモ	*mōtā* *memo*	motor memo, note, list	モットー デモ	*mottō* *demo*	motto demonstration

モ モ モ

モ モ モ

ヤ *ya*	也	-	カヤック シャツ	*kayakku* *shatsu*	kayak undershirt	ジャズ キャベツ	*jazu* *kyabetsu*	jazz cabbage

ヤ ヤ ヤ

ヤ ヤ ヤ

ユ *yu*	由 363	ユニーク *yunīku* unique ニュース *nyūsu* news		ユーモア *yūmoa* humor メニュー *menyū* menu		

ヨ *yo*	與 -	ヨット *yotto* yacht ショー *shō* show		ニューヨーク *Nyū Yōku* New York		

ラ	ra	良	321	ラジオ カラー	*rajio* *karā*	radio color		カメラ グラム	*kamera* *guramu*	camera gram

ラ

リ	ri	利	329	リズム ミリ	*rizumu* *miri*	rhythm millimeter		リスト ベーカリー	*risuto* *bēkarī*	list bakery

リ

| ル ru | 流 247 | ビル | *biru* | building | | ビール | *bīru* | beer |
| | | ホテル | *hoteru* | hotel | | ドル | *doru* | dollar |

ル

| ル | ル | ル | | | | | | |
| | | | | | | | | |

ル	ル	ル											

| レ re | 礼 620 | レコード | *rekōdo* | record | | ステレオ | *sutereo* | stereo |
| | | トイレ | *toire* | toilet | | エレベーター | *erebētā* | elevator |

レ

| レ | レ | レ | | | | | | |
| | | | | | | | | |

レ	レ	レ											

ロ ro	呂	-	ロビー ロシア	*robī* *Roshia*	lobby Russia	ローマじ ゼロ	*rōmaji* *zero*	roman letters zero

ワ wa	和	124	ワープロ タワー	*wāpuro* *tawā*	word processor tower	ワイシャツ シャワー	*waishatsu* *shawā*	shirt shower

| ヲ | o | 乎 | – | シャワー ヲ アビル *shawā o abiru* take a shower |

| ヲ | ヲ | ラ | ラ |

| ヲ | ラ | ラ |

| ン | n | 尓 | – | センター *sentā* center ワイン *wain* wine |
| | | | | パーセント *pāsento* percent コンピュータ *konpyūta* computer |

| ン | ン | ン | ン |

| ン | ン | ン |

1	イ 2a	**JIN, NIN, *hito*** – human being, man, person

アメリカ人　*Amerikajin*　an American
１００人　*hyakunin*　100 people
５，６人　*gorokunin*　5 or 6 people
あの人　*ano hito*　that person, he, she
人々　*hitobito*　people

2	一 1a	***ICHI, ITSU, hito(tsu), hito-*** – – one

一ページ　*ichi pēji*　1 page; page 1
りんご一つ　*ringo hitotsu*　1 apple
一つ一つ　*hitotsu-hitotsu*　one by one, individually
一人　*hitori*　1 person; alone　　1
一人一人　*hitori-hitori*　one by one, one after another　　1

3	一 1a2	**NI, futa(tsu), futa** – two

二人　　　　　*futari, ninin*　2 people　　　　　　　　　　　　　　　　　1
一人二人　　*hitori futari*　1 or 2 people　　　　　　　　　　　　　　2, 1
二人ずつ　　*futarizutsu*　two by two, every 2 people　　　　　　　1
二人とも　　*futaritomo*　both people, both (of them)　　　　　　　1
二けた　　　*futaketa*　2 digits; 2-digit, double-digit

4	一 1a3	**SAN, mit(tsu), mi(tsu), mi** – three

三人　　　　　*sannin*　　　3 people　　　　　　　　　　　　　　　　　1
二, 三人　　*nisannin*　　2 or 3 people　　　　　　　　　　　　　　3, 1
三キロ　　　*sankiro*　　3 kg; 3 km
三つぞろい　*mitsuzoroi*　3-piece suit
二つ三つ　*futatsu mittsu*　2 or 3　　　　　　　　　　　　　　　　　3

5	日 4c	**NICHI, JITSU, hi, -ka** – day; sun		

一 日	*ichinichi, ichijitsu*	1 day	2
	tsuitachi	1st of the month	
二 日	*futsuka*	2 days; 2nd of the month	3
三 日	*mikka*	3 days; 3rd of the month	4
二, 三 日	*nisannichi*	2 or 3 days	3, 4

6	口 ゛ 3s 2o	**SHI, yot(tsu), yo(tsu), yo, yon** – four		

四 人	*yonin*	4 people	1
四 日	*yokka*	4 days; 4th of the month	5
三, 四 日	*san'yokka*	3 or 4 days	4, 5
三, 四 人	*san'yonin*	3 or 4 people	4, 1
四 つんばい	*yotsunbai*	(on) all fours	

7	一 ノ 1a3 1c	***GO, itsu(tsu), itsu*** – five								
		五 人	*gonin*	5 people							1
		五 日	*itsuka*	5 days; 5th of the month							5
		四, 五 日	*shigonichi*	4 or 5 days							6, 5
		四, 五 人	*shigonin*	4 or 5 people							6, 1
		三々五々	*sansan-gogo*	in small groups, by twos and threes							4
五		五	五	五						
五	五	五								

8	一 ゛ 2j 2o	***ROKU, mut(tsu), mu(tsu), mu, [mui]*** – six								
		六 人	*rokunin*	6 people							1
		五, 六 人	*gorokunin*	5 or 6 people							7, 1
		六 日	*muika*	6 days; 6th of the month							5
		五, 六 日	*gorokunichi*	5 or 6 days							7, 5
		六つぐらい	*muttsu-gurai*	about 6							
六		六	六	六						
六	六	六								

9	| ノ 1b 1c	**SHICHI, nana(tsu), nana, [nano]** – seven

七
2 1

七人　　　*shichinin*　　7 people　　　　　　　　　　　1
七日　　　*nanoka*　　　7 days; 7th of the month　　　5
七メートル　*nanamētoru, shichimētoru*　7 meters
七五三　　*Shichigosan*　festival day for 3-, 5-, and 7-year-olds
　　　　　　　　　　　　　　(Nov. 15)　　　　　　　　7, 4

七　七　七

10	＼ ＞ 2o	**HACHI, yat(tsu), ya(tsu), ya, [yō]** – eight

八
1 2

八人　　　*hachinin*　　　8 people　　　　　　　　　　1
八日　　　*yōka*　　　　　8 days; 8th of the month　　5
八ミリ　　*hachimiri*　　　8 mm
八グラム　*hachiguramu*　　8 grams
お八つ　　*oyatsu*　　　　afternoon snack

八　八　八

八　八　八

11	一 丨 1a 1b	**KYŪ, KU, kokono(tsu), kokono** – nine	
		九 人 *kyūnin* 9 people	1
		九 日 *kokonoka* 9 days; 9th of the month	5
		九 ド ル *kyūdoru* 9 dollars	
		九 九 *kuku* multiplication table	

九 九 九

九 九 九

12	十 2k	**JŪ, JI', tō, to** – ten	
		十 人 *jūnin* 10 people	1
		十 日 *tōka* 10 days; 10th of the month	5
		二 十 日 *hatsuka* 20 days; 20th of the month	3, 5
		十 四 日 *jūyokka* 14 days; 14th of the month	6, 5
		十 八 日 *jūhachinichi* 18 days; 18th of the month	10, 5

十 十 十

十 十 十

13	冂 一 丨 2r 1a 1b	**EN** – circle; yen; **maru(i)** – round						
		一 円	*ichien*	1 yen				2
		二 円	*nien*	2 yen				3
		三 円	*san'en*	3 yen				4
		四 円	*yoen*	4 yen				6
		十 円	*jūen, tōen*	10 yen				12

円

14	日 一 ノ 4c 1a 1c	**HYAKU** – hundred				
		百 人	*hyakunin*	100 people		1
		三百六十五日	*sanbyaku rokujūgonichi*	365 days		4, 8, 12, 7, 5
		八 百 円	*happyakuen*	800 yen		10, 13
		九 百	*kyūhyaku*	900		11

百

15	十ノ 2k 1c	**SEN, chi** – thousand			
		一千	*issen*	1,000	2
		三千	*sanzen*	3,000	4
		八千	*hassen*	8,000	10
		千円	*sen'en*	1,000 yen	13
		千人	*sennin*	1,000 people	1

千　千　千

千　千　千

16	一ノ 1a2 1c	**MAN** – ten thousand; **BAN** – many, all			
		一万円	*ichiman'en*	10,000 yen	2, 13
		百万	*hyakuman*	1 million	14
		一千万円	*issenman'en*	10 million yen	2, 15, 13
		二,三万円	*nisanman'en*	20,000-30,000 yen	3, 4, 13
		万一	*man'ichi*	by any chance, should happen to	2

万　万　万

万　万　万

17 月 4b	**GETSU, tsuki** – moon; month; **GATSU** – month								
	一月　　　*ichigatsu*　　January　　　　　　　　　　　　　2								
	hitotsuki　　1 month								
	一か月　　*ikkagetsu*　　1 month　　　　　　　　　　　　2								
	一月八日　*ichigatsu yōka*　January 8　　　　　　　　2, 10, 5								
	月ロケット　*tsuki roketto*　moon rocket								
月	月	月	月						

月	月	月									

18 日 月 4c 4b	**MEI** – light; **MYŌ** – light; next; **a(kari)** – light, clearness; **aka(rui)** – bright; **aki(raka)** – clear; **a(keru), aka(rumu/ramu)** – become light; **a(ku)** – be open; **a(kasu)** – pass (the night); divulge; **a(kuru)** – next, following								
	明日　　　*myōnichi, asu*　tomorrow　　　　　　　　　　5								
	明くる日　*akuruhi*　　the next/following day　　　　　5								
明	明	明							

明	明	明									

19	日 隹 一 4c 8c 1a6	**YŌ** – day of the week		
		曜日	*yōbi*	day of the week	5
		日曜（日）	*nichiyō(bi)*	Sunday	5
		月曜（日）	*getsuyō(bi)*	Monday	17, 5

曜　曜　曜

曜　曜　曜

20	火 4d	**KA, hi, [ho]** – fire		
		火曜（日）	*kayō(bi)*	Tuesday	19, 5
		九月四日（火）	*kugatsu yokka (ka)*	(Tuesday) September 4	11, 6, 17, 5

火　火　火

火　火　火

21	⺡ 3a	***SUI, mizu*** – water

水曜(日)　　*suiyō(bi)*　　Wednesday　　　　　　　　　　　　19, 5
水がめ　　　*mizugame*　　water jug/jar
水かさ　　　*mizukasa*　　volume of water (of a river)

水

水

22	⽊ 4a	***BOKU, MOKU, ki, [ko]*** – tree, wood

木曜(日)　　*mokuyō(bi)*　　Thursday　　　　　　　　　　　　　　19, 5
木こり　　　*kikori*　　woodcutter, lumberjack, logger
木々　　　　*kigi*　　every tree; many trees
千木　　　　*chigi*　　ornamental crossbeams on a Shinto shrine　　15
三木　　　　*Miki*　　(surname)　　　　　　　　　　　　　　　　　　4

木

木

23	金 8a	***KIN, KON*** – gold; metal; money; ***kane*** – money; *[kana]* – metal		
		金曜(日)	*kin'yō(bi)*	Friday 19, 5
		金メダル	*kinmedaru*	gold medal
		金ぱく	*kinpaku*	gold leaf/foil
		金もうけ	*kanemōke*	making money

24	土 3b	***DO, TO, tsuchi*** – earth, soil, ground		
		土曜(日)	*doyō(bi)*	Saturday 19, 5
		土木	*doboku*	civil engineering 22
		土人	*dojin*	native, aborigine 1
		土のう	*donō*	sandbag

25	一 朮 1a 4a	**HON** – book; origin; main; this; (counter of long, thin objects); *moto* – origin		

日 本　　　　　*Nihon, Nippon*　Japan　　　　　　　　　　　　　　5
日 本 人　　　*Nihonjin, Nipponjin*　a Japanese　　　　　　　　5, 1
本 日　　　　　*honjitsu*　today　　　　　　　　　　　　　　　　5
本 土　　　　　*hondo*　mainland　　　　　　　　　　　　　　　24
ビ ー ル 六 本　*bīru roppon*　6 bottles of beer　　　　　　　　　8

26	一 亻 1a 2a	**DAI, TAI**, *ō(kii)*, *ō-* – big, large; *ō(i ni)* – very much, greatly		

大 金　　　　*taikin*　　　large amount of money　　　　　　　23
大 き さ　　　*ōkisa*　　　size
大 水　　　　*ōmizu*　　　flooding, overflow　　　　　　　　　21
大 み そ か　*Ōmisoka*　　New Year's Eve
大 人　　　　*otona*　　　adult　　　　　　　　　　　　　　　1

27	`` ` ` `` 3n	**SHŌ, chii(sai), ko-, o-** – little, small		
		小人	kobito	dwarf, midget	1
			shōjin	insignificant person; small-minded man	
			shōnin	child	
		大小	daishō	large and small; size	26
		小金	kogane	small sum of money; small fortune	23

小　小　小

小　小　小

28	丨口 1b　3s	**CHŪ, naka** – middle; inside; throughout		
		日本中	Nipponjū, Nihonjū	all over Japan	5, 25
		一日中	ichinichijū	all day long	2, 5
		日中	nitchū	during the daytime	5
			Nit-Chū	Japanese-Chinese, Sino-Japanese	
		中小	chūshō	medium and small, smaller, minor	27

中　中　中

中　中　中

29	几 虫 ノ 2s 6d 1c	**FŪ, [FU]** – wind; appearance; style; **kaze, [kaza]** – wind		
		日本風	*nihonfū*	Japanese-style	5, 25
		風土	*fūdo*	natural features, climate	24
		中風	*chūfū, chūbu, chūbū*	paralysis, palsy	28
		そよ風	*soyokaze*	gentle breeze	

風

風 風 風

風 風 風

30	雫 8d	**U, ame, [ama]** – rain		
		風雨	*fūu*	wind and rain	29
		大雨	*ōame*	heavy rain, downpour	26
		小雨	*kosame*	light/fine rain	27
		にわか雨	*niwakaame*	sudden shower	
		雨水	*amamizu*	rainwater	21

雨

雨 雨 雨

雨 雨 雨

| 31 | ├ 一
2m 1a | **KA, GE, shita, moto** – lower, base; **shimo** – lower part; **sa(geru), o(rosu), kuda(su)** – lower, hand down (a verdict); **sa(garu)** – hang down, fall; **o(riru)** – get out of/off (a vehicle); **kuda(ru)** – go/come down; **kuda(saru)** – give |

| 下水 | gesui | sewer system, drainage | 21 |
| 風下 | kazashimo | leeward side | 29 |

| 32 | ├ 一
2m 1a | **JŌ, [SHŌ], ue** – upper; **kami, [uwa-]** – upper part; **a(geru)** – raise; **a(garu), nobo(ru)** – rise; **nobo(seru/su)** – bring up (a topic) |

水上	suijō	on the water	21
上下	jōge	high and low, rise and fall	31
上り下り	noborikudari	ascent and descent, ups and downs	31

33	丨 1b3	**SEN, kawa** – river			
		川上 *kawakami* upstream			32
		川下 *kawashimo* downstream			31
		小川 *ogawa* stream, brook, creek			27
		ミシシッピー川 *Mishishippī-gawa* Mississippi River			
		中川 *Nakagawa* (surname)			28

34	山 3o	**SAN, yama** – mountain			
		山水 *sansui* landscape, natural scenery			21
		火山 *kazan* volcano			20
		下山 *gezan* descent from a mountain			31
		小山 *koyama* hill			27
		山々 *yamayama* mountains			

35	田 5f	**DEN, ta** – rice field, paddy

水田	*suiden*	rice paddy	21
田中	*Tanaka*	(surname)	28
本田	*Honda*	(surname)	25
山田	*Yamada*	(surname)	34
下田	*Shimoda*	(city on Izu Peninsula)	31

36	火 田 4d 5f	**hata, hatake** – cultivated field

| 田畑 | *tahata* | fields | 35 |
| みかん畑 | *mikan-batake* | mandarin orange/tangerine orchard | |

37	刂 2f	**TŌ, katana** – sword, knife								
		日本刀　　*nihontō*　　Japanese sword　　5, 25 大刀　　　*daitō*　　long sword　　26 小刀　　　*shōtō*　　short sword　　27 　　　　　*kogatana*　　knife, pocketknife 山刀　　　*yamagatana*　woodsman's hatchet　　34								

刀

刀	刀	刀							

38	ヽヽ 刂 2o 2f	**BUN** – portion; **BU** – portion, 1 percent; **FUN** – minute (of time/arc); *wa(keru/katsu)* – divide, share, distinguish; *wa(kareru)* – be separated; *wa(karu)* – understand								
		十分　　*jūbun*　enough, sufficient, adequate (cf. No. 828)　12 　　　*jippun*　10 minutes 水分　　*suibun*　water content　　21								

分

分	分	分							

39	刂 一 丨
	2f 1a 1b

SETSU, [SAI], ki(ru) – cut; **ki(reru)** – cut well; break off; run out of

大切	taisetsu	important; precious	26
一切れ	hitokire	slice, piece	2
切り上げ	kiriage	conclusion; rounding up; revaluation	32
切り下げ	kirisage	reduction; devaluation	31

切

切　切　切

切　切　切

40	囗 王 丶
	3s 4f 1d

KOKU, kuni – country

大国	taikoku	large/great country, major power	26
万国	bankoku	all countries, world	16
六か国	rokkakoku	6 countries	8
四国	Shikoku	(one of the 4 main islands of Japan)	6
中国	Chūgoku	China; (region in western Honshu)	28

国

国　国　国

国　国　国

41	土 十 、 3b 2k 1d	**JI, tera** – temple

国分寺　　*Kokubunji*　(common temple name)　　　　40, 38
山寺　　　*yamadera*　mountain temple　　　　　　　34

時	時	時						

42	日 土 十 4c 3b 2k	**JI, toki** – time; hour

四時二十分 *yoji nijippun*　4:20　　　　　　　　6, 3, 12, 38
一時　　　*ichiji*　　　for a time; 1 o'clock　　　　2
　　　　　hitotoki, ittoki　a while, moment
時々　　　*tokidoki*　　sometimes
日時　　　*nichiji*　　 time, date, day and hour　　　5

43 門日 8e 4c	**KAN, KEN, aida** – interval (between); **ma** – interval (between); a room

時 間　　jikan　　　　time; hour　　　　　　　　　　　　　　42
中 間　　chūkan　　　middle, intermediate　　　　　　　　　28
人 間　　ningen　　　human being　　　　　　　　　　　　　1
間 も な く　mamonaku　presently, in a little while, soon

間　間　間

間　間　間

44 一 土 ノ 1a 3b 1c	**SEI, SHŌ** – life; **i(kiru/keru)** – be alive; **i(kasu)** – revive, bring to life; let live; **u(mu)** – bear (a child); **u(mareru)** – be born; **ha(yasu/eru), o(u)** – grow; **nama** – raw, draft (beer); **ki-** – pure

人 生　　jinsei　　　(human) life　　　　　　　　　　　　1
一 生　　isshō　　　 one's whole life　　　　　　　　　　2
生 ビ ー ル　namabīru　draft beer

生　生　生

生　生　生

45	一 ヒ 丨 1a2 2k 1b	**NEN, toshi** – year			
年		生年月日 *seinengappi* date of birth			44, 17, 5
		１９９１年 *sen kyūhyaku kyūjūichinen* 1991			
		五年間 *gonenkan* for 5 years			7, 43
		年金 *nenkin* pension, annuity			23
		三年生 *sannensei* third-year student, junior			4, 44

46	丨 亻 ノ 1b 2a 1c	**I** – (prefix)			
以		以上 *ijō* or more; more than; above-mentioned			32
		三時間以上 *sanjikan ijō* at least 3 hours			4, 42, 43, 32
		以下 *ika* or less; less than; as follows			31
		三つ以下 *mittsu ika* 3 or fewer			4, 31

47	` `丷 月 刂` 2o 4b 2f`	**ZEN, mae** – before, in front of; earlier

以前　　　　　　*izen*　　　　　　ago, previously, formerly　　　　46
前もって　　　　*maemotte*　　　beforehand, in advance
人前 (で)　　　 *hitomae (de)*　 before others, in public　　　　1
分け前　　　　　*wakemae*　　　one's share　　　　　　　　　38
二人前　　　　　*nininmae, futarimae*　enough for 2 people　　3, 1

前　前　前

前　前　前

48	`彳 夂 ノ` 3i 4i 1c2	**GO, nochi** – after, later; **KŌ, ushi(ro)** – behind; *ato* – afterward, subsequent; back, retro-; *oku(reru)* – be late, lag behind

以後　　　　　　*igo*　　　　　　hereafter; since then　　　　　46
前後　　　　　　*zengo*　　　　approximately; front and rear　47
明後日　　　　　*myōgonichi, asatte*　day after tomorrow　　18, 5
その後　　　　　*sonogo*　　　thereafter, later

後　後　後

後　後　後

49	十 一 ノ	**GO** – noon		
	2k 1a 1c	午前	*gozen*	A.M.	47

GO – noon

午前	*gozen*	A.M.	47
午後	*gogo*	afternoon; P.M.	48
午前中	*gozenchū*	all morning, before noon	47, 28
午前も午後も	*gozen mo gogo mo*	both morning and afternoon	47, 48
午後四時	*gogo yoji*	4:00 P.M.	6, 48, 42

午 午 午

午 午 午

50	土 ゛ ノ	**SEN, saki** – earlier; ahead; priority; future; destination; the tip
	3b 2o 1c	

SEN, saki – earlier; ahead; priority; future; destination; the tip

先日	*senjitsu*	recently, the other day	5
先月	*sengetsu*	last month	17
先々月	*sensengetsu*	month before last	17
先生	*sensei*	teacher	44

先 先 先

先 先 先

51	イ 一 2a 1a2	**KON, KIN, ima** – now	
		今日 konnichi, kyō today	5
		今月 kongetsu this month	17
		今年 kotoshi this year	45
		今後 kongo after this, from now on	48
		今ごろ imagoro about this time (of day)	

52	ノ 丶 1c 1d	**NYŪ, hai(ru), i(ru)** – go/come/get in, enter; **i(reru)** – put/let in	
		入国 nyūkoku entry into a country	40
		金入れ kaneire cashbox; purse, wallet	23
		日の入り hi no iri sunset	5
		入り日 irihi setting sun	5

53	＼ 屮 1b2 3o	***SHUTSU, [SUI], da(su)*** – take out; send; ***de(ru)*** – go/come out

出火	*shukka*	outbreak of fire	20
出入り	*deiri*	coming and going (of people)	52
人出	*hitode*	turnout, crowds	1
日の出	*hi no de*	sunrise	5

出　出　出

出　出　出

54	口 3d	***KŌ, KU, kuchi*** – mouth

人口	*jinkō*	population, number of inhabitants	1
入 (り) 口	*iriguchi*	entrance	52
出口	*deguchi*	exit	53
川口	*kawaguchi*	mouth of a river	33
口出し	*kuchidashi*	meddling, butting in	53

口　口　口

口　口　口

55	目 5c

MOKU, [BOKU], me, [ma] – eye; (suffix for ordinals)

一目	*ichimoku, hitome*	a glance	2
人目	*hitome*	notice, public attention	1
目上	*meue*	one's superior/senior	32
目下	*meshita*	one's subordinate/junior	31
	mokka	at present	

56	耳 6e

JI, mimi – ear

耳目	*jimoku*	eye and ear; attention; notice	55
中耳	*chūji*	the middle ear	28
耳たぶ	*mimitabu*	earlobe	

57	扌 3c	**SHU, te, [ta]** – hand

切手　　　*kitte*　　　　(postage) stamp　　　　　　　　　39
小切手　*kogitte*　　　(bank) check　　　　　　　　　27, 39
手本　　*tehon*　　　　model, example, pattern　　　25
上手　　*jōzu*　　　　 skilled, good (at)　　　　　　 32
下手　　*heta*　　　　 unskilled, poor (at)　　　　　 31

58	足 7d	**SOKU, ashi** – foot, leg; **ta(ru/riru)** – be enough, sufficient; **ta(su)** – add up, add (to)

一足　　*issoku*　　　　1 pair (of shoes/socks)　　　　　　2
　　　　hitoashi　　　 a step
手足　　*teashi*　　　　hands and feet, limbs　　　　　　57
足下に　*ashimoto ni*　at one's feet; (watch your) step　31

59	一 丨 ノ 1a4 1b1 1c2	**SHIN, mi** – body			

身上　　　shinjō　　strong point, merit; personal background　32
　　　　　shinshō　one's fortune; property
出 身　　　-shusshin　(be) from ...　53
前 身　　　zenshin　　one's past life; predecessor　47
身 分　　　mibun　　　one's social standing; identity　38

60	亻 木 2a 4a	**KYŪ, yasu(mu)** – rest; **yasu(meru)** – give it a rest; **yasu(maru)** – be rested			

休 日　　　kyūjitsu　　holiday, day off　5
一 休 み　hitoyasumi　short rest　2
中 休 み　nakayasumi　a break, recess　28
休 み 中　yasumichū　Closed (shop sign)　28

61	イ木一 2a 4a 1a	***TAI, TEI, karada*** – body

身体	shintai	body	59
人体	jintai	the human body	1
五体	gotai	the whole body	7
大体	daitai	gist; on the whole, generally	26
風体	fūtei, fūtai	(outward) appearance	29

62	目ノ 5c 1c	***JI, SHI, mizuka(ra)*** – self

自分	jibun	oneself, one's own	38
自身	jishin	oneself, itself	59
自体	jitai	one's own body; itself	61
自国	jikoku	one's own country	40
自らの手で	mizukara no te de	with one's own hands	57

63	目 ヽ 5c 2o	**KEN**, **mi(ru)** – see; **mi(eru)** – be visible; **mi(seru)** – show

一見	ikken	(quick) glance	2
先見	senken	foresight	50
見本	mihon	sample (of merchandise)	25
見出し	midashi	heading, headline	53
見分ける	miwakeru	tell apart, recognize	38

見 見 見

見 見 見

64	門耳 8e 6e	**BUN, MON**, **ki(ku)** – hear; heed; ask; **ki(koeru)** – be audible

見聞	kenbun	information, observation, experience	63
風聞	fūbun	hearsay, rumor	29
聞き手	kikite	listener	57
聞き入れる	kikiireru	accede to, comply with	52

聞 聞 聞

聞 聞 聞

65	耳 又 6e 2h	**SHU, to(ru)** – take			
		取り出す *toridasu*	take out; pick out		53
		取り上げる *toriageru*	take up; adopt; take away		32
		聞き取る *kikitoru*	catch, follow (what someone says)		64
		日取り *hidori*	appointed day		5
		足取り *ashidori*	way of walking, gait		58

66	言 7a	**GEN, GON, -koto** – word; **i(u)** – say			
		一言 *ichigon, hitokoto*	a word, brief comment		2
		一言二言 *hitokoto futakoto*	a word or two		2, 3
		言明 *genmei*	declaration, definite statement		18
		小言 *kogoto*	a scolding; complaints, griping		27
		言い分 *iibun*	one's say; objection		38

67 言 口 一 7a 3d 1a3	**GO** – word; **kata(ru)** – talk, relate; **kata(rau)** – converse					
	日本語　　*Nihongo*　　Japanese language　　　　　　5, 25 国語　　　*kokugo*　　national/Japanese language　　　40 言語　　　*gengo*　　speech, language　　　　　　　　66 一語一語　*ichigo-ichigo*　word for word, verbatim　　2 語り手　　*katarite*　　narrator, storyteller　　　　57					

68 彳 一 丨 3i 1a2 1b	**KŌ, [AN], i(ku), yu(ku)** – go; **GYŌ** – line (of text); **okona(u)** – do, perform, carry out					
	一行　　　*ikkō*　　　　party, retinue　　　　　　　　　2 　　　　　*ichigyō*　　a line (of text) 行間　　　*gyōkan*　　space between lines (of text)　　43 行き先　　*ikisaki, yukisaki*　destination　　　　　　50					

69	一 米 1a 6b	**RAI, ku(ru), kita(ru)** – come; **kita(su)** – bring about

来 年	rainen	next year	45
来 月	raigetsu	next month	17
来 日	rainichi	come to Japan	5
本 来	honrai	originally, primarily	25
以 来	irai	(ever) since	46

70	方 4h	**HŌ** – direction, side; **kata** – direction; person; method

一 方	ippō	on the other hand; only	2
四 方	shihō	north, south, east, west; all directions	6
八 方	happō	all directions, all sides	10
方 言	hōgen	dialect	66
目 方	mekata	weight	55

71	一 木 日 (1a) 4a 4c	**TŌ, higashi** – east		

東方　　　　*tōhō*　　　　the eastward, east　　　　70
中東　　　　*Chūtō*　　　Middle East　　　　28
東大　　　　*Tōdai*　　　University of Tokyo
　　　　　　　　　　　　(abbrev. for 東京大学 *Tōkyō Daigaku*)　26
東アジア　*Higashi Ajia*　East Asia

72	一 口 ◟◞ 1a 3s 2o	**SEI, SAI, nishi** – west		

西方　　　　*seihō*　　　　　　the westward, west　　　70
東西　　　　*tōzai*　　　　　　east and west　　　　　71
西風　　　　*seifū, nishikaze*　westerly wind　　　　　29
西日　　　　*nishibi*　　　　　the afternoon sun　　　　5
西ヨーロッパ　*Nishi Yōroppa*　Western Europe

73	一 卜 丨 1a 2m 1b	**HOKU, kita** – north

北 北 北

北方	*hoppō*	the northward, north	70
北風	*hokufū, kitakaze*	wind from the north	29
東北	*Tōhoku*	(region in northern Honshu)	71
北東	*hokutō*	northeast	71
北北東	*hokuhokutō*	north-northeast	71

北 北 北

74	十 冂 ヽヽ 2k2 2r 2o	**NAN, [NA], minami** – south

南 南 南

西南	*seinan*	southwest	72
東南アジア	*Tōnan Ajia*	Southeast Asia	71
南北	*nanboku*	south and north, north-south	73
南アルプス	*Minami Arupusu*	Southern (Japan) Alps	
南口	*minamiguchi*	southern entrance/exit	54

南 南 南

75	一 厂 丨 1a2 2p 1b	**SA, hidari** – left

左 方	*sahō*	left side	70
左 手	*hidarite*	left hand; (on) the left	57
左 足	*hidariashi*	left foot/leg	58
左 目	*hidarime*	left eye	55
左 上	*hidariue*	upper left	32

76	口 厂 3d 2p	**U, YŪ, migi** – right

右 方	*uhō*	right side	70
左 右	*sayū*	left and right; control	75
右 手	*migite*	right hand; (on) the right	57
右 足	*migiashi*	right foot/leg	58
右 から 左 へ	*migi kara hidari e*	from right to left; quickly	75

77	ᵎ 一 3n 1a3	**TŌ, a(teru/taru)** – hit, be on target

当

本当	hontō	truth; really	25
当時	tōji	at present; at that time	42
当分	tōbun	for now, for a while	38
手当て	teate	allowance, compensation; medical treatment	57
一人当たり	hitoriatari	per person, per capita	2, 1

78	石 5a	**SEKI, [SHAKU], ishi** – stone; **[KOKU]** – (unit of volume, about 180 liters)

石

石けん	sekken	soap	
木石	bokuseki	trees and stones; inanimate objects	22
小石	koishi	small stone, pebble	27
石切り	ishikiri	stonecutting, quarrying	39

79	牛 一 ノ 4g 1a 1c3	**BUTSU, MOTSU, mono** – object, thing		
		人 物	*jinbutsu*	person, personage	1
		生 物	*seibutsu*	living beings, life	44
		見 物	*kenbutsu*	sightseeing	63
		物 語	*monogatari*	tale, story	67
		本 物	*honmono*	genuine, the real thing	25

80	一 口 十 1a3 3s 2k	**JI, [ZU], koto** – thing, affair		
		人 事	*jinji*	human/personnel affairs	1
		火 事	*kaji*	a fire	20
		事 前/後	*jizen/go*	before/after the fact	47, 48
		大 事	*daiji*	great thing, important	26
		出 来 事	*dekigoto*	event, occurrence	53, 69

81	、 ク	***SEKI, yū*** – evening		
	1d 2n	一 夕	*isseki*	one evening	2
		夕 方	*yūgata*	evening	70
		夕 日	*yūhi*	evening/setting sun	5
		夕 月	*yūzuki*	evening moon	17
		七 夕	*tanabata*	Star Festival (July 7)	9

82	口 ク 、	***MEI, MYŌ, na*** – name, reputation		
	3d 2n 1d	人 名	*jinmei*	name of person	1
		名 人	*meijin*	master, expert, virtuoso	1
		名 物	*meibutsu*	noted product (of a locality)	79
		大 名	*daimyō*	(Japanese) feudal lord	26
		名 前	*namae*	a name	47

83	ト ケ 、 2m 2n 1d	***GAI, GE, soto*** – outside; ***hoka*** – other; ***hazu(reru/su)*** – slip off; miss

外 (国) 人	*gai(koku)jin*	foreigner	40, 1
外 来 語	*gairaigo*	word of foreign origin, loanword	69, 67
外 出	*gaishutsu*	go out	53
以 外	*igai*	besides, except (for)	46

84	一 亻 冂 (1a) 2a 2r	***NAI, [DAI], uchi*** – inside

国 内	*kokunai*	domestic, internal	40
体 内	*tainai*	inside the body	61
内 外	*naigai*	inner and outer; domestic and foreign	83
年 内 に	*nennai ni*	before the year is out	45
一 年 以 内 に	*ichinen inai ni*	within a year	2, 45, 46

85	一 ク ト (1a) 2n 2m	**SHI** – death; **shi(nu)** – die

死体　　shitai　　dead body, corpse　　61
死人　　shinin　　dead person, the dead　　1
死後　　shigo　　after death　　48
水死　　suishi　　drowning　　21
死語　　shigo　　dead language　　67

死　死　死

死　死　死

86	阝 立 口 2d 5b 3d	**BU** – part, section; copy of a publication

一部　　　ichibu　　a part　　2
部分　　　bubun　　a part　　38
大部分　　daibubun　greater part, most　　26, 38
本部　　　honbu　　headquarters　　25
北部　　　hokubu　the north (of a country)　　73

部　部　部

部　部　部

87	イ 立 口 2a 5b 3d	**BAI** – double, times, -fold

倍

一 倍	*ichibai*	as much again	2
二 倍	*nibai*	double, twice as much	3
三 倍	*sanbai*	3 times as much, threefold	4
三 倍 以 上	*sanbai ijō*	at least 3 times as much	4, 46, 32
倍 に す る	*bai ni suru*	double	

88	一 十 丿 1a 2k 1c	**HAN, naka(ba)** – half

半

半 分	*hanbun*	half	38
半 年	*hantoshi*	half a year, 6 months	45
三 時 半	*sanjihan*	3:30	4, 42
前 半	*zenhan, zenpan*	first half	47
大 半	*taihan*	greater part, majority	26

89	亻 王 2a 4f	**ZEN, matta(ku)** – all, whole, entirely

全部   *zenbu*   all   86
全国   *zenkoku*   the whole country   40
全体   *zentai*   the whole, (in) all   61
全身   *zenshin*   the entire body   59
万全   *banzen*   perfect, absolutely sure   16

全 全 全

90	口 口 3s 3d	**KAI, [E]** – times, repetitions; **mawa(su)** – send around, rotate; **mawa(ru)** – go around, revolve

十回   *jikkai*   10 times   12
今/前回   *kon/zenkai*   this/last time   51, 47
言い回し   *iimawashi*   expression, turn of phrase   66
上回る   *uwamawaru*   be more than, exceed   32

回 回 回

91	冂土口 2r 3b 3d	***SHŪ, mawa(ri)*** – lap, circumference; surroundings		
		一周	*isshū*	1 lap, 1 revolution	2
		半周	*hanshū*	semicircle, halfway around	88
		円周	*enshū*	circumference of a circle	13
		百周年	*hyakushūnen*	100th anniversary	14, 45

周

92	⻌土口 2q 3b 3d	***SHŪ*** – week		
		二週間	*nishūkan*	2 weeks	3, 43
		先週	*senshū*	last week	50
		今週	*konshū*	this week	51
		来週	*raishū*	next week	69
		週日	*shūjitsu*	weekday	5

週

93	火 艹 一	**MU, BU, na(i)** – not be; (prefix) un-, without, -less		
	4d 3k 1a2	無名	*mumei*	anonymous; unknown	82

無名　　*mumei*　　anonymous; unknown　　82
無口　　*mukuchi*　　taciturn, laconic　　54
無言　　*mugon*　　silent, mute　　66
無休　　*mukyū*　　no holidays, always open (shop)　　60
無事　　*buji*　　safe and sound　　80

94	一 丨 ノ	**FU, BU** – (prefix) not, un-		
	1a 1b 1c			

不足　　*fusoku*　　insufficiency, shortage　　58
不十分　　*fujūbun*　　not enough, inadequate　　12, 38
行方不明　　*yukue fumei*　　whereabouts unknown, missing　　68, 70, 18
不当　　*futō*　　improper, unjust　　77
不死身　　*fujimi*　　invulnerable　　85, 59

95	一 卜 丨 1a3 2m 1b	**CHŌ** – long; chief, head; **naga(i)** – long		
		部長	buchō	department head, director	86
		身長	shinchō	person's height	59
		長時間	chōjikan	long time, many hours	42, 43
		長年	naganen	many/long years	45
		長い間	nagai aida	for a long time	43

長　長　長

長　長　長

96	一 ゛ ノ 1a3 2o 1c2	**HATSU, HOTSU** – emit; start from; depart		
		発明	hatsumei	invention	18
		発見	hakken	discovery	63
		発行	hakkō	publish, issue	68
		出発	shuppatsu	departure, start out	53
		発足	hossoku	start, inauguration	58

発　発　発

発　発　発

97	心 4k

SHIN, kokoro – heart, mind; core

中心	chūshin	center, midpoint	28
心身	shinshin	body and mind/spirit	59
本心	honshin	one's right mind; real intention	25
内心	naishin	one's inmost heart, true intent	84
一心に	isshin ni	with singlehearted devotion, fervently	2

心 心 心

心 心 心

98	心 土 一 4k 3b 1a

SEI – sex; nature (of); **SHŌ** – temperament

中性	chūsei	neuter gender	28
性行	seikō	character and conduct	68
発がん性	hatsugansei	carcinogenic, cancer-causing	96
性分	seibun	nature, temperament	38
本性	honshō, honsei	true nature/character	25

性 性 性

性 性 性

99	囲 心 5f 4k	**SHI, omo(u)** – think, believe	
		思 い 出 *omoide* memories	53
		思 い 出 す *omoidasu* remember	53
		思 い 切 って *omoikitte* resolutely, daringly	39
		思 い や り *omoiyari* compassion, considerateness	
		思 い 上 がった *omoiagatta* conceited, cocky	32

思　思　思　思

思　思　思

100	力 2g	**RYOKU, RIKI, chikara** – force, power	
		体 力 *tairyoku* physical strength	61
		水 力 *suiryoku* water/hydraulic power	21
		風 力 *fūryoku* force of the wind	29
		全 力 *zenryoku* all one's power, utmost efforts	89
		無 力 *muryoku* powerless, helpless	93

力　力　力

力　力　力

101	田 力 5f 2g

DAN, NAN, otoko – man, human male

男性	dansei	man; masculine gender	98
長男	chōnan	eldest son	95
男の人	otoko no hito	man	1
山男	yamaotoko	mountain dweller; mountaineer	34
大男	ōotoko	giant, tall man	26

102	女 3e

JO, NYO, [NYŌ], onna – woman; **me** – feminine

女性	josei	woman; feminine gender	98
長女	chōjo	eldest daughter	95
男女	danjo	men and women	101
女中	jochū	maid	28
女の人	onna no hito	woman	1

103 子 2c	**SHI, SU, ko** – child		
	男子	*danshi*	boy, man	101
	男の子	*otoko no ko*	boy	101
	女子	*joshi*	girl, woman	102
	女の子	*onna no ko*	girl	102
	分子	*bunshi*	molecule; numerator of a fraction	38

子　子　子

子　子　子

104 好 3e 2c	**KŌ, kono(mu), su(ku)** – like		
	好物	*kōbutsu*	favorite food	79
	好人物	*kōjinbutsu*	good-natured person	1, 79
	物好き	*monozuki*	idle curiosity	79
	好き好き	*sukizuki*	matter of individual preference	
	大好き	*daisuki*	like very much	26

好　好　好

好　好　好

105	宀 女 3m 3e	**AN** – peace, peacefulness; *yasu(i)* – cheap		
		安心	*anshin*	feel relieved/reassured	97
		安全	*anzen*	safety	89
		不安	*fuan*	unease, anxiety, fear	94
		目安	*meyasu*	standard, yardstick	55
		安物	*yasumono*	cheap goods	79

106	宀 木 女 3m 4a 3e	**AN** – plan, proposal		
		案内	*annai*	guidance, information	84
		案外	*angai*	contrary to expectations	83
		名案	*meian*	good idea	82
		思案	*shian*	consideration, reflection	99
		案出	*anshutsu*	contrive, devise	53

107	冂 十 一 2r 2k 1a	**YŌ** – business; usage; **mochi(iru)** – use		
		用事	yōji	business affair; errand	80
		用水	yōsui	city/tap water	21
		用語	yōgo	(technical) term, vocabulary	67
		無用	muyō	useless; unnecessary	93
		男子用	danshiyō	for men, men's	101, 103

用

用	用	用					

用	用	用									

108	雨 日 丨 8d 4c 1b	**DEN** – electricity		
		電力	denryoku	electrical power/energy	100
		電子	denshi	electron	103
		発電	hatsuden	generation of electricity	96
		外電	gaiden	telegram from abroad	83

電

電	電	電					

電	電	電									

109	ⸯ 宀 子 3n 2i 2c	**GAKU** – science, study; **mana(bu)** – learn		

大学　　　*daigaku*　　university, college　　　　　　　26
学部　　　*gakubu*　　academic department; faculty　86
入学　　　*nyūgaku*　entry/admission into a school　52
学生　　　*gakusei*　　student　　　　　　　　　　　44
語学　　　*gogaku*　　linguistics　　　　　　　　　　67

学 学 学

学 学 学

110	宀 子 3m 2c	**JI** – character, letter; **aza** – village section		

国字　　　　*kokuji*　　national/Japanese script　　　　　　40
当て字　　　*ateji*　　　kanji used phonetically/for meaning　77
ローマ字　*rōmaji*　roman letters
字体　　　　*jitai*　　　form of a character, type font　　　　61
十字　　　　*jūji*　　　a cross　　　　　　　　　　　　　　12

字 字 字

字 字 字

111	亠ノヽ 2j 1c 1d	**BUN, MON** – literature, text, sentence; **fumi** – letter, note		
		文字	*moji, monji*	letter, character	110
		文学	*bungaku*	literature	109
		本文	*honbun, honmon*	text, wording	25
		文語	*bungo*	the written language	67
		文明	*bunmei*	civilization	18

文

112	一ノヽ 1a2 1c 1d2	**BO, haha** – mother		
		母子	*boshi*	mother and child	103
		生母	*seibo*	one's biological mother	44
		母国語	*bokokugo*	one's mother tongue	40, 67
		母方	*hahakata*	on the mother's side, maternal	70
		お母さん	*okāsan*	mother	

母

113	` ` ノ ` ` 2o 1c 1d	**FU, chichi** – father

父母　　*fubo*　　　father and mother　　　112
父子　　*fushi*　　　father and child/son　　103
父方　　*chichikata*　on the father's side, paternal　70
父上　　*chichiue*　　father　　　　　　　　　32
お父さん　*otōsan*　　father

父　父　父

父　父　父

114	亠 `丷` ノ 2j 2o 1c	**KŌ** – intersection; coming and going; **ma(jiru/zaru)** – (intr.) mix; **maji(eru)**, **ma(zeru)** – (tr.) mix; **maji(waru), ka(u)** – associate (with); **ka(wasu)** – exchange (greetings)

国交　　*kokkō*　　　diplomatic relations　　　　40
外交　　*gaikō*　　　foreign policy, diplomacy　　83
性交　　*seikō*　　　sexual intercourse　　　　　98

交　交　交

交　交　交

115	木 亠 ソ 4a 2j 2o	**KŌ** – school; (printing) proof

校

学 校	gakkō	school	109
小 学 校	shōgakkō	elementary school	27, 109
中 学 校	chūgakkō	junior high school	28, 109
母 校	bokō	alma mater	112
校 長	kōchō	principal, headmaster	95

校 校 校

校 校 校

116	一 ノ 1a3 1c3	**MAI** – every, each

毎

毎 年	mainen, maitoshi	every year, yearly, annual	45
毎 月	maigetsu, maitsuki	every month, monthly	17
毎 週	maishū	every week, weekly	92
毎 日	mainichi	every day, daily	5
毎 時	maiji	every hour, hourly, per hour	42

毎 毎 毎

毎 毎 毎

117	氵 一 ノ 3a 1a3 1c3	**KAI, umi** – sea, ocean

大 海	*taikai*	an ocean	26
海 上	*kaijō*	ocean, seagoing, marine	32
海 外	*kaigai*	overseas, abroad	83
内 海	*uchiumi, naikai*	inland sea	84
日 本 海	*Nihonkai*	Sea of Japan	5, 25

118	土 丨 ノ 3b 1b2 1c	**CHI, JI** – earth, land

土 地	*tochi*	land, soil	24
地 下	*chika*	underground, subterranean	31
地 方	*chihō*	region, area	70
地 名	*chimei*	place name	82
生 地	*kiji*	material, cloth	44

119	シ 丨 ノ 3a 1b2 1c	**CHI, ike** – pond		
		用水池	*yōsuichi*	water reservoir	107, 21
		電池	*denchi*	battery	108
		池田	*Ikeda*	(surname)	35

120	イ 丨 ノ 2a 1b2 1c	**TA** – other, another		
		他人	*tanin*	another person; stranger	1
		他国	*takoku*	another/foreign country	40
		他方	*tahō*	the other side/party/direction	70
		自他	*jita*	oneself and others	62
		その他	*sonota*	and so forth	

121	立 5b	***RITSU, [RYŪ], ta(tsu)*** – stand (up); ***ta(teru)*** – set up, raise		
		国立	*kokuritsu*	national, state-supported	40
		自立	*jiritsu*	independent, self-supporting	62
		中立	*chūritsu*	neutral, neutrality	28
		目立つ	*medatsu*	be conspicuous, stick out	55
		立ち上がる	*tachiagaru*	stand up	32

立　立　立

立　立　立

122	亻立 2a 5b	***I, kurai*** – rank, position		
		地位	*chii*	position, rank	118
		学位	*gakui*	academic degree	109
		上位	*jōi*	higher rank	32
		本位	*hon'i*	monetary standard; basis, principle	25
		位取り	*kuraidori*	position (before/after decimal point)	65

位　位　位

位　位　位

123 氵 土 ノ 3a 3b 1c	**HŌ, HA', HO' –** law			
	国法	kokuhō	laws of the country	40
	立法	rippō	enactment of legislation	121
	法案	hōan	bill, legislative proposal	106
	文法	bunpō	grammar	111
	方法	hōhō	method	70

法　法　法

法　法　法

124 禾 口 5d 3d	**WA, [O] –** peace, harmony; *yawa(rageru/ragu), nago(mu)* – soften, calm down; *nago(yaka)* – mild, gentle, congenial			
	和文	wabun	Japanese script	111
	和風	wafū	Japanese style	29
	不和	fuwa	disharmony, discord, enmity	94
	大和	Yamato	(old) Japan	26

和　和　和

和　和　和

125	禾 ノ 丶 5d 1c 1d	**SHI, watakushi** – I; private		
		私事	*shiji*	personal affairs	80
		私物	*shibutsu*	private property	79
		私用	*shiyō*	private use	107
		私立	*shiritsu*	private, privately supported	121
		私自身	*watakushi jishin*	personally, as for me	62, 59

私　私　私

私　私　私

126	丷 ノ 丶 2o 1c 1d	**KŌ, ōyake** – public, official		
		公安	*kōan*	public peace/security	105
		公法	*kōhō*	public law	123
		公立	*kōritsu*	public	121
		公海	*kōkai*	international waters	117
		公言	*kōgen*	public declaration, avowal	66

公　公　公

公　公　公

127	木 4a2	**RIN, hayashi** – woods, forest

山林	sanrin	mountains and forests; mountain forest	34
(山)林学	(san)ringaku	forestry	34, 109
林立	rinritsu	stand close together in large numbers	121
小林	Kobayashi	(surname)	27

128	木 4a3	**SHIN, mori** – woods, forest

| 森林 | shinrin | woods, forest | 127 |
| 大森 | Ōmori | (area of Tokyo) | 26 |

129	⺮ 6f	**CHIKU, take** – bamboo

竹 林	*chikurin, takebayashi*	bamboo grove/thicket	127
竹 刀	*shinai*	bamboo sword (for Kendo)	37
さ お 竹	*saodake*	bamboo pole	
竹 の つ え	*take no tsue*	bamboo cane	
竹 や ぶ	*takeyabu*	bamboo thicket	

130	⺮ 十 一 6f 2k 1a4	**HITSU, fude** – writing brush

万 年 筆	*mannenhitsu*	fountain pen	16, 45
自 筆	*jihitsu*	one's own handwriting; autograph	62
筆 名	*hitsumei*	pen name, pseudonym	82
文 筆	*bunpitsu*	literary work, writing	111
筆 先	*fudesaki*	tip of the writing brush	50

131	日 土 一 4c 3b 1a3	**SHO, ka(ku)** – write

書物　　　shomotsu　　book　　　　　　　　　　　　79
文書　　　bunsho　　　(in) writing, document　　　111
書名　　　shomei　　　book title　　　　　　　　　　82
前書き　　maegaki　　foreword, preface　　　　　　47
書き取り　kakitori　　dictation　　　　　　　　　　65

132	立 日 心 5b 4c 4k	**I** – will, heart, mind, thought; meaning, sense

意見　　　iken　　　opinion　　　　　　　　　　　　　　　63
用意　　　yōi　　　　preparations, readiness　　　　　　107
好意　　　kōi　　　　goodwill, good wishes, kindness　　104
意外　　　igai　　　unexpected, surprising　　　　　　　83
不意　　　fui　　　　sudden, unexpected　　　　　　　　94

133 車 7c	**SHA, kuruma** – vehicle; wheel		
	電車	*densha*	electric train	108
	人力車	*jinrikisha*	rickshaw	1, 100
	発車	*hassha*	departure	96
	下車	*gesha*	get off (a train)	31
	水車	*suisha*	waterwheel	21

134 一ノ、 1a3 1c2 1d	**KI, KE** – spirit, soul, mood		
	人気	*ninki*	popularity	1
	気分	*kibun*	feeling, mood	38
	本気	*honki*	seriousness, (in) earnest	25
	気体	*kitai*	a gas	61
	電気	*denki*	electricity	108

| 135 | 氵 一 丿
3a 1a3 1c | **KI** – steam
汽車　　kisha　　train drawn by steam locomotive | 133 |

汽　汽　汽

汽　汽　汽

136	厂 日 灬 2p 4c 3n	**GEN** – original, fundamental; **hara** – plain, field; wilderness	
		原案　　　gen'an　　　the original plan/proposal	106
		原書　　　gensho　　　(in) the original (text)	131
		原文　　　genbun　　　the text, the original	111
		原生林　　genseirin　　primeval/virgin forest	44, 127
		原子　　　genshi　　　atom	103

原　原　原

原　原　原

137	一　ゝ 1a2　2o	**GEN** – yuan, yüan (Chinese monetary unit); **GAN, moto** – origin, foundation		
		元日	*ganjitsu*	New Year's Day	5
		元金	*gankin*	principal (vs. interest)	23
		元気	*genki*	healthy, peppy	134
		地元	*jimoto*	local	118

元　元　元

元　元　元

138	゛　ゝ　一 3n　2o　1a	**KŌ, hikari** – light; **hika(ru)** – shine		
		日光	*nikkō*	sunlight, sunshine	5
		月光	*gekkō*	moonlight	17
		光年	*kōnen*	light-year	45
		発光	*hakkō*	luminosity, emit light	96
		電光	*denkō*	electric light, lightning	108

光　光　光

光　光　光

139	一 丨 1a2　1b	***KŌ, KU*** – artisan; manufacturing, construction

工事 (中)	*kōji(chū)*	(under) construction	80, 28
大 工	*daiku*	carpenter	26
女 工	*jokō*	woman factory-worker	102
工 学	*kōgaku*	engineering	109
人 工	*jinkō*	man-made, artificial	1

工　工　工

工　工　工

140	宀 ソ 一 3m　2o　1a2	***KŪ, sora*** – sky; ***a(keru/ku)*** – make/be unoccupied; ***kara*** – empty

空 気	*kūki*	air	134
(時 間 と) 空 間	*(jikan to) kūkan*	(time and) space	42, 43
空 車	*kūsha*	empty car, For Hire (taxi)	133
空 手	*karate*	empty-handed; karate	57
大 空	*ōzora*	sky, firmament	26

空　空　空

空　空　空

141	一 イ 1a2 2a	**TEN, ame, [ama]** – heaven

天気	*tenki*	weather	134
天文学	*tenmongaku*	astronomy	111, 109
天国	*tengoku*	paradise	40
天性	*tensei*	nature, natural constitution	98
天の川	*amanogawa*	Milky Way	33

142	一 日 土 (1a) 4c 3b	**RI** – (old unit of length, about 2.9 km); **sato** – village; one's parents' home

千里	*senri*	1,000 *ri*; a great distance	15
海里	*kairi*	nautical mile	117
里子	*satogo*	foster child	103
里心	*satogokoro*	homesickness	97

143	王 日 土 4f 4c 3b	**RI** – reason, logic, principle	
		地理 (学) *chiri(gaku)* geography	118, 109
		心理学 *shinrigaku* psychology	97, 109
		理学部 *rigakubu* department of science	109, 86
		無理 *muri* unreasonable; impossible; (by) force	93
		理事 *riji* director	80

144	⸌ ノ 3n 1c	**SHŌ**, *suko(shi)* – a little; *suku(nai)* – little, few, slight	
		少年 *shōnen* boy	45
		少年法 *shōnenhō* the Juvenile Law	45, 123
		少女 *shōjo* girl	102
		少々 *shōshō* a little	
		少しずつ *sukoshizutsu* little by little, a little at a time	

145	目 `` ノ 5c 3n 1c

SEI, kaeri(miru) – reflect upon, give heed to; ***SHŌ*** – (government) ministry;
habu(ku) – omit; cut down on

自省	*jisei*	reflection, introspection	62
内省	*naisei*	introspection	84
人事不省	*jinjifusei*	unconsciousness, fainting	1, 80, 94
文部省	*Monbushō*	Ministry of Education	111, 86

146	朩 目 4a 5c

SŌ – aspect, phase; ***SHŌ*** – (government) minister; ***ai-*** – together, fellow, each
other

相当	*sōtō*	suitable, appropriate	77
文相	*bunshō*	minister of education	111
外相	*gaishō*	foreign minister	83
相手	*aite*	the other party, partner, opponent	57

147	忄目木 4k 5c 4a	**SŌ, [SO]** – idea, thought		
		思想	shisō	idea, thought	99

		思想	shisō	idea, thought	99
		回想	kaisō	retrospection, reminiscence	90
		理想	risō	an ideal	143
		空想	kūsō	fantasy, daydream	140
		めい想	meisō	meditation	

想

148	丷目一 2o 5c 1a	**SHU, kubi** – neck, head		

首相	shushō	prime minister	146
元首	genshu	sovereign, ruler	137
首位	shui	leading position, top spot	122
部首	bushu	radical of a kanji	86
手首	tekubi	wrist	57

首

149	辶目 ヽヽ 2q 5c 2o	**DŌ, [TŌ], michi** – street, way, path

道

	国 道	kokudō	national highway	40
	水 道	suidō	water conduits, running water	21
	北 海 道	Hokkaidō	(northernmost of the 4 main islands	73, 117
	書 道	shodō	calligraphy ⌊of Japan)	131
	回 り 道	mawarimichi	a detour	

道 道 道

道 道 道

150	辶冂十 2q 2r 2k	**TSŪ, [TSU], tō(ru)** – go through, pass; **tō(su)** – let through; **kayo(u)** – commute

通

	交 通	kōtsū	traffic, transportation	114
	文 通	buntsū	correspondence, exchange of letters	111
	通 学	tsūgaku	attend school	109
	見 通 し	mitōshi	prospects, outlook	63

通 通 通

通 通 通

151	足 攵口 7d 4i 3d	**RO, -ji** – street, way		

路

	道路	*dōro*	street, road	149
	十字路	*jūjiro*	intersection, crossroads	12, 110
	水路	*suiro*	waterway, aqueduct	21
	海路	*kairo*	sea route	117
	通路	*tsūro*	passageway, walkway, aisle	150

路	路	路							

路	路	路							

152	戸 4m	**KO, to** – door		

戸

	戸外で	*kogai de*	outdoors, in the open air	83
	下戸	*geko*	nondrinker, teetotaler	31
	戸口	*toguchi*	doorway	54
	木戸	*kido*	gate, entrance; castle gate	22
	雨戸	*amado*	storm door, shutter	30

戸	戸	戸							

戸	戸	戸							

153	戸 厂 一	**SHO, tokoro** – place

4m	2p	1a

案内所	annaijo	inquiry office, information desk	106, 84
名所	meisho	noted place, sights (to see)	82
所長	shochō	director, head, manager	95
長所	chōsho	strong point, merit, advantage	95
発電所	hatsudensho	power plant	96, 108

154	土 日 一	**JŌ, ba** – place

3b	4c	1a2

工場	kōjō, kōba	factory, plant	139
出場	shutsujō	stage appearance; participation	53
場所	basho	place, location	153
立ち場	tachiba	standpoint, point of view	121
相場	sōba	market price	146

155	主 、 4f 1d	**SHU, [SU], nushi** – lord, master; main; **omo** – main, principal

主人	shujin	husband, head of household	1
主人公	shujinkō	hero, main character	1, 126
自主	jishu	independence, autonomy	62
主語	shugo	subject (in grammar)	67
地主	jinushi	landowner, landlord	118

156	亻 主 、 2a 4f 1d	**JŪ, su(mu/mau)** – live, dwell, reside

住所	jūsho	an address	153
住人	jūnin	inhabitant, resident	1
安住	anjū	peaceful living	105
住まい	sumai	residence, where one lives, address	
住み心地	sumigokochi	comfortableness, livability	97, 118

157	イ 言 2a 7a	**SHIN** – faith, trust, belief			
		信用	shin'yō	trust	107
		不信	fushin	bad faith, insincerity; distrust	94
		自信	jishin	(self-)confidence	62
		所信	shoshin	one's conviction, opinion	153
		通信	tsūshin	communication, correspondence, dispatch	150

158	イ 一 ノ 2a 1a2 1c	**KAI** – meeting; association; **E, a(u)** – meet			
		国会	kokkai	parliament, diet, congress	40
		大会	taikai	mass meeting; sports meet, tournament	26
		学会	gakkai	learned/academic society	109
		会見	kaiken	interview, news conference	63
		出会う	deau	happen to meet, run into	53

159	イ 口 一 2a 3d 1a	**GŌ, GA', [KA'], a(u)** – fit; **a(waseru/wasu)** – put together	

合意 　　 gōi 　　　 mutual consent, agreement 　　　132
場合 　　 baai, bawai 　(in this) case 　　　　　　154
(お)見合い (o)miai 　 marriage interview 　　　　　63
見合わせる miawaseru 　look at each other; postpone 　63
間に合う ma ni au 　　 be in time (for); will do, suffice 　43

160	⺮ 口 イ 6f 3d 2a	**TŌ, kota(e)** – an answer; **kota(eru)** – answer	

回答 　　 kaitō 　　 an answer, reply 　　　　90
口答 　　 kōtō 　　　 oral answer 　　　　　　54
筆答 　　 hittō 　　　 written answer 　　　　130
名答 　　 meitō 　　　 correct answer 　　　　82
答案 　　 tōan 　　　 examination paper 　　　106

161 門 8e	**MON, kado** – gate		
	入門(書)	*nyūmon(sho)*	introduction, primer	52, 131
	部門	*bumon*	group, category, branch	86
	名門	*meimon*	distinguished/illustrious family	82
	門下生	*monkasei*	(someone's) pupil	31, 44
	門口	*kadoguchi*	front door, entrance	54

162 門口 8e 3d	**MON, to(i), [ton]** – question, problem; **to(u)** – matter, care about		
	問答	*mondō*	questions and answers, dialogue	160
	学問	*gakumon*	learning, science	109
	問い合わせる	*toiawaseru*	inquire, ask	159
	問いただす	*toitadasu*	inquire, question	

133

163 口 貝 3d 7b	**IN** – member			
	会 員	*kaiin*	member (of a society)	158
	海 員	*kaiin*	seaman, sailor	117
	工 員	*kōin*	factory worker	139
	人 員	*jin'in*	staff, personnel	1
	全 員	*zen'in*	all members, entire staff	89

164 日 土 ノ 4c 3b 1c	**SHA, mono** – person			
	学 者	*gakusha*	scholar	109
	日 本 学 者	*Nihongakusha*	Japanologist	5, 25, 109
	筆 者	*hissha*	writer, author	130
	信 者	*shinja*	believer, the faithful	157
	後 者	*kōsha*	the latter	48

165	宀 一 ノ 3m 1a 1c4	**KA, KE**, *ie, ya* – house; family

家 事   *kaji*   family affairs; household chores   80
家 内   *kanai*   (one's own) wife   84
家 来   *kerai*   retainer, vassal   69
国 家   *kokka*   state, nation   40
家 主   *yanushi*   landlord, house owner   155

家

166	宀 土 一 3m 3b 1a	**SHITSU** – a room; *muro* – greenhouse; cellar

和 室   *washitsu*   Japanese-style room   124
私 室   *shishitsu*   private room   125
室 内   *shitsunai*   in a room, indoor   84
分 室   *bunshitsu*   isolated room; annex   38
室 長   *shitsuchō*   senior roommate; section chief   95

室

167	尸 土 一 3r 3b 1a	**OKU, ya** – roof, house; shop, dealer			
		家 屋	kaoku	house, building	165
		屋 上	okujō	roof, rooftop	32
		部 屋	heya	a room	86
		小 屋	koya	cottage, hut, shack	27
		八 百 屋	yaoya	vegetable shop, greengrocer	10, 14

屋

屋 屋 屋

屋 屋 屋

168	广 口 卜 3q 3d 2m	**TEN, mise** – shop, store			
		書 店	shoten	bookstore	131
		本 店	honten	head office, main shop	25
		店 員	ten'in	store employee, clerk	163
		店 先	misesaki	storefront	50
		出 店	demise	branch store	53

店

店 店 店

店 店 店

169	├ 火 口 2m 4d 3d	**TEN** – point

出 発 点　*shuppatsuten*　starting point　53, 96
原 点　*genten*　starting point; origin (of coordinates)　136
合 点　*gaten, gatten*　understanding; consent　159
点 字　*tenji*　Braille　110
点 火　*tenka*　ignite　20

170	尸 口 一 3r 3d 1a	**KYOKU** – bureau, office

当 局　*tōkyoku*　the authorities, responsible officials　77
局 長　*kyokuchō*　director of a bureau; postmaster　95
局 員　*kyokuin*　staff member of a bureau　163
局 外 者　*kyokugaisha*　outsider, onlooker　83, 164
時 局　*jikyoku*　the situation　42

171 戸口十 3r 3d 2k	**KYO, i(ru)** – be (present), exist			
	住居	*jūkyo*	dwelling, residence	156
	居住地	*kyojūchi*	place of residence	156, 118
	居間	*ima*	living room	43
	長居	*nagai*	stay (too) long	95
	居合わせる	*iawaseru*	(happen to) be present	159

172 十口 2k 3d	**KO, furu(i)** – old; **furu(su)** – wear out			
	古風	*kofū*	old customs; antiquated	29
	古語	*kogo*	archaic word; old adage	67
	古文	*kobun*	classical literature, ancient classics	111
	古今東西	*kokon-tōzai*	all ages and countries	51, 71, 72
	古本	*furuhon*	secondhand/used book	25

173	夂口 十 4i 3d 2k	**KO** – deceased; **yue** – reason, cause; circumstances		

故人	kojin	the deceased	1
故事	koji	historical	80
事故	jiko	accident	80
故国	kokoku	one's homeland, native country	40
故意	koi	intention, purpose	132

174	立 木 厂 5b 4a 2p	**SHIN**, **atara(shii)**, **ara(ta)**, **nii-** – new		

新聞	shinbun	newspaper	64
古新聞	furushinbun	old newspapers	172
新年	shinnen	the New Year	45
新人	shinjin	newcomer, new face	1
一新	isshin	renovation, reform	2

175	立 目 木 5b 5c 4a	**SHIN** – intimacy; parent; **oya** – parent; **shita(shii)** – intimate, close (friend); **shita(shimu)** – get to know better

親切	shinsetsu	kind, friendly	39
親日	shin-Nichi	pro-Japanese	5
母親	hahaoya	mother	112
親子	oyako	parent and child	103

176	貝 厂 一 7b 2p2 1a2	**SHITSU** – quality, nature; **SHICHI, [CHI]** – hostage; pawn

質問	shitsumon	a question	162
性質	seishitsu	nature, property	98
物質	busshitsu	matter, material, substance	79
本質	honshitsu	essence, substance	25
人質	hitojichi	hostage	1

177	一 尸 、 1a 3r 1d	**MIN, tami** – people, nation					
		国民	kokumin	people, nation, citizen			40
		人民	jinmin	the people, citizens			1
		(原)住民	(gen)jūmin	(aboriginal) native of a place			136, 156
		民間	minkan	private (not public)			43
		民意	min'i	will of the people			132

民

| 宅 |

178	宀 ｜ ノ 3m 1b 1c2	**TAKU** – house, home, residence					
		住宅	jūtaku	house, residence			156
		自宅	jitaku	one's own home, private residence			62
		私宅	shitaku	one's private residence			125
		宅地	takuchi	land for housing, residential site			118
		家宅	kataku	house, the premises			165

宅

179	宀 日 イ 3m 4c 2a	**SHUKU, yado** – lodging, inn; **yado(ru)** – take shelter; be pregnant; **yado(su)** – give shelter; conceive (a child)

下 宿	geshuku	room and board; boardinghouse	31
合 宿	gasshuku	lodging together	159
民 宿	minshuku	private house providing tourist lodging	177
宿 屋	yadoya	inn	167

180	糸 厂 一 6a 2p 1a	**SHI, kami** – paper

和 紙	washi	Japanese paper	124
日 本 紙	nihonshi	Japanese paper	5, 25
新 聞 紙	shinbunshi	newspaper; newsprint	174, 64
質 問 用 紙	shitsumon yōshi	questionnaire	176, 162, 107
手 紙	tegami	letter	57

181	亠巾 2j 3f	**SHI** – city; **ichi** – market			

市長　shichō　mayor　95
市会　shikai　municipal assembly, city council　158
市立　shiritsu　municipal　121
市民　shimin　citizen, townspeople　177
市場　ichiba, shijō　marketplace, market　154

182	田 一 丨 5f 1a 1b	**CHŌ, machi** – town, quarter			

町民　chōmin　townsman, townsfolk　177
町人　chōnin　merchant; townsfolk　1
町内　chōnai　neighborhood　84
下町　shitamachi　(low-lying) downtown area　31
室町　Muromachi　(historical period, 1392–1573)　166

183	匚ノ、 2t 1c 1d	**KU** – municipal administrative district, ward						

地区　　　*chiku*　　district, area, zone　　118
区間　　　*kukan*　　section, interval　　43
区切る　　*kugiru*　　partition; punctuate　　39
区分　　　*kubun*　　division, partition; classification　　38
北区　　　*Kita-ku*　　Kita Ward (Tokyo)　　73

区　区　区

区　区　区

184	一丨 1a 1b	**CHŌ** – even number; (counter for blocks of houses/blocks of tofu/guns/dishes of prepared food); **TEI** – D, No. 4 (in a series); adult; ⊤ shape						

丁目　　　*chōme*　　city block (in addresses)　　55
丁年　　　*teinen*　　(age of) majority, adulthood　　45
丁字路　　*teijiro*　　⊤-shaped street intersection　　110, 151

丁　丁　丁

丁　丁　丁

185	米 田 ノ
	6b 5f 1c

BAN – keeping watch; number, order

一番	ichiban	the first; number one, most	2
二番目	nibanme	the second, No. 2	3, 55
番地	banchi	lot/house number	118
局番	kyokuban	exchange (part of a phone number)	170
交番	kōban	police box	114

186	彳 土 一
	3i 3b2 1a2

GAI, [KAI], machi – street

街路	gairo	street	151
街道	kaidō	street, highway	149
市街	shigai	the streets (of a city); town	181
名店街	meitengai	arcade of well-known stores	82, 168
地下街	chikagai	underground shopping mall	118, 31

187	彳 木 一 3i 4a 1a2	**JUTSU** – art, technique; means; conjury

手術　　　　　*shujutsu*　　(surgical) operation　　　　　　57
手術室　　　*shujutsushitsu*　operating room　　　　　57, 166
学術　　　　*gakujutsu*　　science, learning　　　　　　109
(学)術(用)語　*(gaku)jutsu(yō)go*　technical term, terminology 109, 107, 67

術

188	阝 日 土 2d 4c 3b	**TO, TSU, miyako** – capital (city)

(大)都市　*(dai)toshi*　(major/large) city　　　　26, 181
都会　　*tokai*　　city　　　　　　　　　158
首都　　*shuto*　　capital (city)　　　　　148
都内　　*tonai*　　in (the city of) Tokyo　　84
都合　　*tsugō*　　circumstances, reasons　　159

都

189	亠 口 丷	**KYŌ, KEI** – the capital
	2j 3d 3n	

東京 (都)	*Tōkyō(-to)*	(City of) Tokyo	71, 188
京都 (市)	*Kyōto(-shi)*	(City of) Kyoto	188, 181
上京	*jōkyō*	go/come to Tokyo	32
北京	*Pekin*	Peking, Beijing	73
南京	*Nankin*	Nanking	74

京 京 京

京 京 京

190	亠 口 冂	**KŌ, taka(i)** – high; expensive; **taka** – amount, quantity; **taka(maru)** – rise;
	2j 3d2 2r	**taka(meru)** – raise

高原	*kōgen*	plateau, heights, tableland	136
高校	*kōkō*	senior high school (cf. No. 569)	115
名高い	*nadakai*	renowned, famous	82

高 高 高

高 高 高

147

191	木 十 、 4a 2k 1d	**SON, mura** – village

市町村	shichōson	cities, towns, and villages	181, 182
村会	sonkai	village assembly	158
村長	sonchō	village mayor	95
村民	sonmin	villager	177
村人	murabito	villager	1

192	亻 十 、 2a 2k 1d	**FU, tsu(ku)** – be attached, belong (to); **tsu(keru)** – attach, apply (cf. No. 1843)

交付	kōfu	deliver, hand over	114
日付け	hizuke	date (of a letter)	5
気付く	kizuku	(take) notice	134
付き物	tsukimono	what (something) entails, adjunct	79

193	阝 口 厂	**GUN** – county, district		
	2d 3d 2p	郡部	*gunbu*	rural district	86
		新田郡	*Nitta-gun*	Nitta District (in Gunma Prefecture)	174, 35

郡　郡　郡

郡　郡　郡

194	⌙ 目 丨	**KEN** – prefecture, province		
	3n 5c 1b	郡県	*gunken*	districts/counties and prefectures	193
		県立	*kenritsu*	prefectural, provincial	121
		県道	*kendō*	prefectural highway	149
		県会	*kenkai*	prefectural assembly	158
		山口県	*Yamaguchi-ken*	Yamaguchi Prefecture	34, 54

県　県　県

県　県　県

195	リ丨丶 2f 1b2 1d2	**SHŪ** – state, province; **su** – sandbank, shoals		
		本州	Honshū	(largest of the 4 main islands of Japan)	25

州

		カリフォルニア州	Kariforunia-shū	(State of) California	
		五大州	godaishū	Asia, Africa, Europe, America, and Australia	7, 26
		中州	nakasu	sandbank in a river	28

196	丗丷一 3k 2o 1a	**KYŌ, tomo** – together, both, all		
		共学	kyōgaku	coeducation	109

共

		共通	kyōtsū	(in) common (with)	150
		公共	kōkyō	the public, community	126
		共和国	kyōwakoku	republic	124, 40

197	イ 艹 ソ 2a 3k 2o	**KYŌ, [KU], tomo** – retinue, attendant; serve; **sona(eru)** – offer

供出   *kyōshutsu*   delivery   53
自供   *jikyō*   confession, admission   62
供物   *kumotsu*   votive offering   79
子供   *kodomo*   child   103
(お)供   *(o)tomo*   accompany (someone)

198	冂 口 一 2r 3d 1a	**DŌ, ona(ji)** – same

同時に   *dōji ni*   at the same time, simultaneously   42
共同   *kyōdō*   joint, communal, cooperative   196
合同   *gōdō*   combination, merger, joint   159
同意   *dōi*   agreement, consent   132
同居   *dōkyo*   live in the same house   171

199	口 冂 ノ 3d 2r 1c	**KŌ, mu(kau)** – face (toward); proceed (to); **mu(ku/keru)** – (intr./tr.) turn; **mu(kō)** – opposite side

方向	*hōkō*	direction	70
向上	*kōjō*	elevation, betterment	32
意向	*ikō*	intention, inclination	132
外人向け	*gaijinmuke*	for foreigners	83, 1

200	一 业 冂 1a 3o 2r	**RYŌ** – both; (obsolete Japanese coin)

両親	*ryōshin*	parents	175
両方	*ryōhō*	both	70
両手	*ryōte*	both hands	57
両立	*ryōritsu*	coexist, be compatible (with)	121
車両	*sharyō*	car, vehicle	133

201

氵 艹 山
3a 3k 3o

満

MAN, mi(chiru) – become full; **mi(tasu)** – fill; fulfill

満足	*manzoku*	satisfaction	58
不満	*fuman*	dissatisfaction, discontent	94
満員	*man'in*	full to capacity	163
満点	*manten*	perfect score	169
円満	*enman*	harmonious, peaceful, perfect	13

202

十 一 ノ
2k 1a 1c

平

HEI, BYŌ, tai(ra), hira – flat, level

平行	*heikō*	parallel	68
平和	*heiwa*	peace	124
不平	*fuhei*	discontent, complaint	94
平家	*Heike*	(historical clan name)	165
	hiraya	1-story house	

203	宀 亻 一 3m 2a 1a3	**JITSU** – truth, actuality; **mi** – fruit, nut; **mino(ru)** – bear fruit		
		事実	jijitsu	fact	80
		口実	kōjitsu	pretext, excuse	54
		実行	jikkō	put into practice, carry out, realize	68
		実力	jitsuryoku	actual ability, competence	100
		実用	jitsuyō	practical use	107

実

204	⼓ 一 丨 2n 1a2 1b2	**SHOKU, SHIKI, iro** – color; erotic passion		
		原色	genshoku	primary color	136
		好色	kōshoku	sensuality, lust, eroticism	104
		色紙	shikishi	(type of calligraphy paper)	180
			irogami	colored paper	
		金色	kin'iro, kinshoku, konjiki gold color		23

色

205	日 ノ 4c 1c	**HAKU, BYAKU, shiro(i), shiro, [shira]** – white

白紙	hakushi	white/blank paper	180
白書	hakusho	a white paper (on), report	131
白人	hakujin	a white, Caucasian	1
自白	jihaku	confession, admission	62
空白	kūhaku	a blank; vacuum	140

206	火 日 土 4d 4c 3b	**KOKU, kuro(i), kuro** – black

黒人	kokujin	a black, Negro	1
黒白	kuroshiro, kokubyaku	black and/or white; right and wrong	205
黒字	kuroji	(in the) black, black figures	120
黒子	kuroko	black-clad Kabuki stagehand	103

207	土 丨 ノ 3b 1b2 1c	*SEKI, [SHAKU], aka(i), aka* – red; *aka(ramu)* – become red, blush; *aka(rameru)* – make red, blush		
		赤十字　　*Sekijūji*　　Red Cross		12, 110
		赤道　　　*sekidō*　　equator		149
		赤字　　　*akaji*　　deficit, red figures, (in the) red		110
		赤ちゃん　*akachan*　baby		

208	月 土 一 4b 3b 1a	*SEI, [SHŌ], ao(i), ao* – blue, green; unripe		
		青年　　　　*seinen*　　young man/people		45
		青少年　　　*seishōnen*　young people, youth		144, 45
		青空　　　　*aozora*　blue sky		140
		青空市場　　*aozora ichiba*　open-air market		140, 181, 154
		青物　　　　*aomono*　green vegetables		79

209	心 月 土 4k 4b 3b	**JŌ, [SEI], nasa(ke)** – emotion, sympathy; circumstances		
		人 情	*ninjō*	human feelings, humanity	1
		同 情	*dōjō*	sympathy	198
		無 情	*mujō*	heartlessness, callousness	93
		事 情	*jijō*	circumstances, situation	80
		実 情	*jitsujō*	actual situation, the facts	203

210	日 一 ノ 4c 1a 1c2	**TEKI** – (attributive suffix); **mato** – target		
		目 的	*mokuteki*	purpose, aim, goal	55
		一 時 的	*ichijiteki*	temporary	2, 42
		民 主 的	*minshuteki*	democratic	177, 155
		理 想 的	*risōteki*	ideal	143, 147
		自 発 的	*jihatsuteki*	voluntary, spontaneous	62, 96

211	糸 一 |	***YAKU*** – approximately; promise	
	6a 1a 1b	公約　　　*kōyaku*　　public commitment	126
		口約　　　*kōyaku*　　verbal promise	54
		先約 (が あ る)　*sen'yaku (ga aru)*　(have a) previous engagement	50
		約半分　*yaku hanbun*　approximately half	88, 38
		約三キロ　*yaku sankiro*　approximately 3 km/kg	4

約

約　約　約

約 約 約

212	弓	***KYŪ, yumi*** – bow (for archery/violin)	
	3h	弓術　　　*kyūjutsu*　　(Japanese) archery	187
		弓道　　　*kyūdō*　　　(Japanese) archery	149

弓

弓　弓　弓

弓 弓 弓

213	一 亻 ノ 1a2　2a　1c	**SHI, ya** – arrow		
		弓矢	*yumiya*	bow and arrow	212

矢　矢　矢

矢　矢　矢

214	口 亻 一 3d　2a　1a2	**CHI, shi(ru)** – know

通知	*tsūchi*	a notification, communication	150
周知	*shūchi*	common knowledge, generally known	91
知事	*chiji*	governor (of a prefecture)	80
知人	*chijin*	an acquaintance	1
知り合い	*shiriai*	an acquaintance	159

知　知　知

知　知　知

215	口 亻 丷 3d 2a 2o	**TAN, mijika(i)** – short			
短		長短	*chōtan*	(relative) length; good and bad points	95
		短刀	*tantō*	short sword, dagger	37
		短気	*tanki*	short temper, touchiness, hastiness	134
		短所	*tansho*	defect, shortcoming	153
		短大	*tandai*	junior college (cf. No. 449)	26

216	弓 丨 3h 1b	**IN, hi(ku)** – pull; attract; **hi(keru)** – be ended; make cheaper			
引		引力	*inryoku*	attraction, gravitation	100
		引用	*in'yō*	quotation, citation	107
		引き出し	*hikidashi*	drawer	53
		取り引き	*torihiki*	transaction, trade	65
		引き上げ	*hikiage*	raise, increase	32

217	弓 虫 ノ	***KYŌ, GŌ, tsuyo(i)*** – strong; ***tsuyo(maru)*** – become strong(er); ***tsuyo(meru)*** – make strong(er), strengthen; ***shi(iru)*** – force
	3h 6d 1c	

強力	*kyōryoku*	strength, power	100
強国	*kyōkoku*	strong country, great power	40
強情	*gōjō*	stubbornness, obstinacy	209
強引に	*gōin ni*	by force	216

強　強　強

強　強　強

218	弓 冫	***JAKU, yowa(i)*** – weak; ***yowa(ru/maru)*** – become weak(er); ***yowa(meru)*** – make weak(er), weaken
	3h2 2b2	

強弱	*kyōjaku*	strengths and weaknesses, strength	217
弱点	*jakuten*	a weakness, weak point	169
弱体	*jakutai*	weak	61
弱気	*yowaki*	faintheartedness; bearishness (of market)	134

弱　弱　弱

弱　弱　弱

219	犭 虫 3g 6d	**DOKU, hito(ri)** – alone		
		独立	*dokuritsu*	independence	121
		独身	*dokushin*	unmarried, single	59
		独学	*dokugaku*	self-study	109
		日独	*Nichi-Doku*	Japan and Germany, Japanese-German	5
		和独	*Wa-Doku*	Japanese-German (dictionary)	124

独

独　独　独

独　独　独

220	匚 亻 一 2t 2a 1a2	**I** – medicine, healing		
		医学	*igaku*	medicine	109
		医学部	*igakubu*	medical department/school	109, 86
		医学用語	*igaku yōgo*	medical term	109, 107, 67
		医者	*isha*	physician, doctor	164
		女医	*joi*	woman physician, lady doctor	102

医

医　医　医

医　医　医

221	方 亻 一 4h 2a 1a3	**ZOKU** – family, tribe			
		家族	*kazoku*	family	165
		親族	*shinzoku*	relative, kin	175
		一族	*ichizoku*	one's whole family, kin	2
		部族	*buzoku*	tribe	86
		民族	*minzoku*	race, people, nation	177

族

222	方 厂 一 4h 2p 1a	**RYO, tabi** – trip, travel			
		旅行	*ryokō*	trip, travel	68
		旅行者	*ryokōsha*	traveler, tourist	68, 164
		旅人	*tabibito*	traveler, wayfarer	1
		旅先	*tabisaki*	destination	50
		旅立つ	*tabidatsu*	start on a journey	121

旅

223	イ冂 2a2 2r	**NIKU** – meat, flesh			

肉屋	nikuya	butcher (shop)	167
肉体	nikutai	the body, the flesh	61
肉親	nikushin	blood relationship/relative	175
肉付きのよい	nikuzuki no yoi	well-fleshed, plump	192
肉筆	nikuhitsu	one's own handwriting; autograph	130

224	米 6b	**BEI, MAI, kome** – rice			

白米	hakumai	polished rice	205
新米	shimai	new rice; novice	174
外米	gaimai	imported rice	83
日米	Nichi-Bei	Japan and America, Japanese-U.S.	5
南米	Nanbei	South America	74

225	攵米女 4i 6b 3e	**SŪ, [SU], kazu** – number; **kazo(eru)** – count		
		数字	*sūji*	digit, numeral, figures	110
		数学	*sūgaku*	mathematics	109
		人数	*ninzū*	number of people	1
		無数	*musū*	countless, innumerable	93
		手数	*tesū*	trouble, bother	57

226	頁米 亻 9a 6b 2a	**RUI** – kind, type, genus		
		親類	*shinrui*	relative, kin	175
		人類	*jinrui*	mankind	1
		書類	*shorui*	papers, documents	131
		分類	*bunrui*	classification	38
		類語	*ruigo*	synonym	67

227	一 車 ノ 1a 7c 1c	**JŪ, CHŌ, omo(i)** – heavy; **kasa(naru/neru)** – lie/pile on top of one another; **-e** – -fold, -ply

体 重	taijū	body weight	61
重 力	jūryoku	gravity, gravitation	100
重 大	jūdai	weighty, grave, important	26
二 重	nijū, futae	double, twofold	3

228	禾 車 一 5d 7c 1a	**SHU** – kind, type; seed; **tane** – seed; species; cause

種 類	shurui	kind, type, sort	226
一 種	isshu	kind, sort	2
人 種	jinshu	a human race	1
種 子	shushi	seed, pit	103
不 安 の 種	fuan no tane	cause of unease	94, 105

229

1d2 2n2

TA, ō(i) – much, many, numerous

多少	tashō	much or little, many or few; some	144
多数	tasū	large number (of); majority	225
大多数	daitasū	the overwhelming majority	26, 225
多元的	tagenteki	pluralistic	137, 210
数多く	kazuōku	many, great number (of)	225

230

3d3

HIN – refinement; article; **shina** – goods, quality

上品	jōhin	refined, elegant, graceful	32
下品	gehin	unrefined, gross, vulgar	31
品質	hinshitsu	quality	176
部品	buhin	(spare/machine) parts	86
品物	shinamono	merchandise	79

231	力 車 ノ 2g 7c 1c2	**DŌ, ugo(ku/kasu)** – (intr./tr.) move		
		自動車	*jidōsha*	automobile, car	62, 133
		動物	*dōbutsu*	animal	79
		動力	*dōryoku*	moving force, (electric) power	100
		行動	*kōdō*	action	68
		動員	*dōin*	mobilize	163

動

232	イ 車 力 2a 7c 2g	**DŌ, hatara(ku)** – work		
		実働時間	*jitsudōjikan*	actual working hours	203, 42, 43
		働き	*hataraki*	work; functioning; ability	
		働き口	*hatarakiguchi*	job, position	54
		働き者	*hatarakimono*	hard worker	164
		働き手	*hatarakite*	worker, breadwinner; capable man	57

働

233	⺍ 冖 力 3n 2i 2g	**RŌ** – labor, toil		
		労働	*rōdō*	work, labor	232
		労働者	*rōdōsha*	worker, laborer	232, 164
		労働時間	*rōdō jikan*	working hours	232, 42, 43
		労力	*rōryoku*	trouble, effort; labor	100
		心労	*shinrō*	worry, concern	97

労

234	十 力 2k 2g3	**KYŌ** – cooperation		
		協力	*kyōryoku*	cooperation	100
		協力者	*kyōryokusha*	collaborator, coworker	100, 164
		協同	*kyōdō*	cooperation, collaboration, partnership	198
		協会	*kyōkai*	society, association	158
		日米協会	*Nichi-Bei Kyōkai*	the America-Japan Society	5, 224, 158

協

235	夂 力 一 4i 2g 1a2	**MU, tsuto(meru)** – work, serve		
		事務所	jimusho	office	80, 153
		公務員	kōmuin	government employee	126, 163
		国務	kokumu	affairs of state	40
		外務省	Gaimushō	Ministry of Foreign Affairs	83, 145
		法務省	Hōmushō	Ministry of Justice	123, 145

務

236	一 日 土 1a 4c 3b	**YA, no** – field, plain		
		野生	yasei	wild (animal/plant)	44
		平野	heiya	a plain	202
			Hirano	(surname)	
		分野	bun'ya	field (of endeavor)	38
		野原	nohara	field, plain	136

野

237	氵 口 十 3a 3d 2k	**KATSU** – life, activity		
		生活	seikatsu	life	44
		活発	kappatsu	active, lively	96
		活動	katsudō	activity	231
		活用	katsuyō	practical use; conjugate, inflect	107
		活字	katsuji	printing/movable type	110

活

238	言 口 十 7a 3d 2k	**WA, hanashi** – conversation, story; **hana(su)** – speak		
		会話	kaiwa	conversation	158
		電話	denwa	telephone	108
		立ち話	tachibanashi	chat while standing	121
		話し手	hanashite	speaker	57
		話し合う	hanashiau	talk over, discuss	159

話

239	売 亠ー丷 3p 2i 2o	**BAI, u(ru)** – sell; **u(reru)** – be sold

売店　　　baiten　　　stand, newsstand, kiosk　　　168
売り子　　uriko　　　store salesclerk　　　103
売り手　　urite　　　seller　　　57
売り切れ　urikire　　sold out　　　39
小売り　　kouri　　　retailing, retail　　　27

240	貝 7b	**kai** – shellfish (cf. No. 453)

貝類　　　　kairui　　　shellfish (plural)　　　226
ほら貝　　　horagai　　trumpet shell, conch
貝ボタン　　kaibotan　shell button

241	罒貝 5g 7b	**BAI, ka(u)** – buy

売買　　　　baibai　　buying and selling, trade, dealing　　239
買い物　　　kaimono　shopping, purchase　　　79
買い手　　　kaite　　buyer　　　57
買い主　　　kainushi　buyer　　　155
買い入れる　kaiireru　purchase, stock up on　　52

242	糸 6a	**SHI, ito** – thread

一糸まとわぬ　isshi matowanu　stark naked　　　2
糸口　　　itoguchi　　end of a thread; beginning; clue　　54
糸車　　　itoguruma　spinning wheel　　　133
糸目　　　itome　　a fine thread　　　55
生糸　　　kiito　　raw silk　　　44

243	糸 圭 宀 6a 3p 2i	**ZOKU, tsuzu(ku/keru)** – (intr./tr.) continue		
		続出	zokushutsu	appear one after another	53
		続行	zokkō	continuation	68
		相続	sōzoku	succession; inheritance	146
		手続き	tetsuzuki	procedures, formalities	57
		引き続いて	hikitsuzuite	continuously, uninterruptedly	216

244	言 圭 宀 7a 3p 2i	**DOKU, TOKU, [TŌ], yo(mu)** – read		
		読者	dokusha	reader	164
		読書	dokusho	reading	131
		読本	tokuhon	reader, book of readings	25
		読み物	yomimono	reading matter	79
		読み方	yomikata	reading, pronunciation (of a word)	70

245	攵 土 子 4i 3b 2c	**KYŌ, oshi(eru)** – teach; **oso(waru)** – be taught, learn		
		教室	kyōshitsu	classroom	166
		教員	kyōin	teacher, instructor; teaching staff	163
		教会	kyōkai	church	158
		回教	kaikyō	Islam, Muhammadanism	90
		教え方	oshiekata	teaching method	70

246	亠 月 ノ 2j 4b 1c	**IKU, soda(tsu)** – grow up; **soda(teru)** – raise		
		教育	kyōiku	education	245
		体育	taiiku	physical education	61
		発育	hatsuiku	growth, development	96
		生育	seiiku	growth, development	44
		育ての親	sodate no oya	foster/adoptive parent	175

247	氵 亠 丨 3a 2j 1b3	**RYŪ** – a current; style, school (of thought); **[RU]**, **naga(reru)** – flow; **naga(su)** – pour

流 通　　ryūtsū　　circulation, distribution, ventilation　　150
海 流　　kairyū　　ocean current　　117
流 行　　ryūkō　　fashion, fad, popularity　　68
一 流　　ichiryū　　first class　　2

248	日 十 4c 2k	**SŌ**, **[SA']**, **haya(i)** – early; fast; **haya(maru)** – be hasty; **haya(meru)** – hasten

早 々　　sōsō　　early, immediately
早 目 に　　hayame ni　　a little early (leaving leeway)　　55
早 耳　　hayamimi　　quick-eared, in the know　　56
手 早 い　　tebayai　　quick, nimble, agile　　57

249	艹 日 十 3k 4c 2k	**SŌ**, **kusa** – grass, plants

草 原　　sōgen　　grassy plain, grasslands　　136
草 木　　sōmoku, kusaki　　plants and trees, vegetation　　22
草 本　　sōhon　　herb　　25
草 書　　sōsho　　(cursive script form of kanji)　　131
草 案　　sōan　　(rough) draft　　106

250	艹 一 丶 3k 1a 1d	**shiba** – lawn

芝 生　　shibafu　　lawn　　44
芝 草　　shibakusa　　lawn　　249
人 工 芝　　jinkō shiba　　artficial turf　　1, 139
芝 居　　shibai　　stage play, theater　　171
芝 居 小 屋　　shibai-goya　　playhouse, theater　　171, 27, 167

251	艹 木 亻 3k 4a 2a	**CHA, SA** – tea		
		茶色	*chairo*	brown	204
		茶畑	*chabatake*	tea plantation	36
		茶室	*chashitsu*	tea-ceremony room	166
		茶の間	*cha no ma*	living room	43
		茶道	*chadō, sadō*	tea ceremony	149

252	一 艹 丨 1a 3k 1b	**SEI, SE, yo** – world, era		
		二世	*nisei*	second generation	3
		中世	*chūsei*	Middle Ages	28
		世間	*seken*	the world, public, people	43
		出世	*shusse*	success in life, getting ahead	53
		世話	*sewa*	taking care of, looking after	238

253	艹 木 一 3k2 4a 1a	**YŌ, ha** – leaf, foliage		
		葉書	*hagaki*	postcard	131
		青葉	*aoba*	green foliage	208
		言葉	*kotoba*	word; language	66
		木の葉	*ko no ha*	tree leaves, foliage	22
		千葉	*Chiba*	(prefecture east of Tokyo)	15

254	亻 卜 2a 2m	**KA, KE, ba(keru)** – turn oneself (into); **ba(kasu)** – bewitch		
		文化	*bunka*	culture	111
		化学	*kagaku*	chemistry	109
		強化	*kyōka*	strengthening	219
		合理化	*gōrika*	rationalization, streamlining	159, 143
		化け物	*bakemono*	spook, ghost, monster	79

255	艹 イ ト 3k 2a 2m	**KA, hana** – flower, blossom

草花	kusabana	flower, flowering plant	249
生け花	ikebana	flower arranging	44
花屋	hanaya	flower shop, florist	167
花見	hanami	viewing cherry blossoms	63
花火	hanabi	fireworks	20

花　花　花

花花花

256	イ 戈 2a 4n	**DAI** – generation; age; price; **TAI, ka(waru)** – represent; **ka(eru)** – replace; **yo** – generation; **shiro** – price; substitution

時代	jidai	era, period	42
古代	kodai	ancient times, antiquity	172
世代	sedai	generation	252
代理	dairi	representation; agent	143

代　代　代

代代代

257	亠 夂 丨 2j 4i 1b2	**HEN, ka(waru/eru)** – (intr./tr.) change

変化	henka	change, alteration	254
変動	hendō	change, fluctuation	231
変種	henshu	variety, strain	228
変人	henjin	an eccentric	1
不変	fuhen	immutability, constancy	94

変　変　変

変変変

258	亠 心 丨 2j 4k 1b2	**REN, koi** – (romantic) love; **ko(u)** – be in love; **koi(shii)** – dear, fond, long for

恋人	koibito	boyfriend, girlfriend, lover	1
恋文	koibumi	love letter	111
恋心	koigokoro	(awakening of) love	97
道ならぬ恋	michi naranu koi	forbidden love	149

恋　恋　恋

恋恋恋

259	夂 心 ⺍ 4i 4k 3n	**AI** – love

恋 愛	*ren'ai*	love	258
愛 情	*aijō*	love	209
愛 国 心	*aikokushin*	patriotic sentiment, patriotism	40, 97
愛 読	*aidoku*	like to read	244
愛 想	*aisō*	amiability, sociability	147

260	又 ⺍ ⼍ 2h 3n 2i	**JU, u(keru)** – receive; **u(karu)** – pass (an exam)

受 理	*juri*	acceptance	143
受 動	*judō*	passive	231
受 け 身	*ukemi*	passivity; passive (in grammar)	59
受 (け) 付 (け)	*uketsuke*	receptionist, reception desk	192
受 け 取 る	*uketoru*	receive, accept, take	65

261	戈 一 ｜ 4n 1a 1b	**SEI, [JŌ], na(ru)** – become; consist (of); **na(su)** – do; form

成 長	*seichō*	growth	95
成 年	*seinen*	(age of) majority, adulthood	45
成 立	*seiritsu*	establishment, founding	121
合 成	*gōsei*	composition, synthesis	159
成 り 行 き	*nariyuki*	course (of events), development	68

262	心 戈 口 4k 4n 3d	**KAN** – feeling, sensation

五 感	*gokan*	the 5 senses	7
感 心	*kanshin*	admire	97
感 想	*kansō*	one's thoughts, impressions	147
感 情	*kanjō*	feelings, emotion	209
感 受 性	*kanjusei*	sensibility, sensitivity	260, 98

263	日 耳 又 4c 6e 2h	**SAI, motto(mo)** – highest, most

最後　saigo　end; last　48
最新　saishin　newest, latest　174
最大　saidai　maximum, greatest, largest　26
最高　saikō　maximum, highest, best　190
最上　saijō　best, highest　32

264	又 厂 2h 2p	**YŪ, tomo** – friend

友人　yūjin　friend　1
学友　gakuyū　fellow student, classmate; alumnus　109
親友　shin'yū　close friend　175
友好　yūkō　friendship　104
友情　yūjō　friendliness, friendship　209

265	月 厂 4b 2p	**YŪ, U, a(ru)** – be, exist, have

国有　kokuyū　state-owned　40
私有　shiyū　privately owned　125
所有　shoyū　possession, ownership　153
有名　yūmei　famous　82
有力　yūryoku　influential, powerful　100

266	口 一 ノ 3d 1a 1c	**GŌ** – number; pseudonym

番号　bangō　(identification) number　185
三号室　sangōshitsu　Room No. 3　4, 166
年号　nengō　name/year of a reign era　45
信号　shingō　signal　157
号外　gōgai　an extra (edition of a newspaper)　83

176

267	刂口一 2f 3d 1a	**BETSU** – different, separate; another, special; *waka(reru)* – diverge, part, bid farewell

別

区別	kubetsu	difference, distinction	183
分別	funbetsu	discretion, good judgment	38
別人	betsujin	different person	1
別居	bekkyo	(legal) separation; live separately	171

268	土厂丨 3b 2p 1b	**ZAI** – outskirts, country; be located; *a(ru)* – be, exist

在

所在地	shozaichi	(prefectural) capital, (country) seat; location	153, 118
在日	zainichi	(stationed) in Japan	5
在外	zaigai	overseas, abroad	83
不在	fuzai	absence	94

269	子厂丨 2c 2p 1b	**SON, ZON** – exist; know, believe

存

存在	sonzai	existence	268
生存	seizon	existence, life	44
存続	sonzoku	continuance, duration	243
共存	kyōson, kyōzon	coexistence	196
存分に	zonbun ni	as much as one likes, freely	38

270	夂土一 4i 3b 1a	**BAKU, mugi** – wheat, barley, rye, oats

麦

小麦	komugi	wheat	27
大麦	ōmugi	barley	26
麦畑	mugibatake	wheat field	36
麦わら	mugiwara	(wheat) straw	
麦茶	mugicha	wheat tea, barley water	251

177

271 糸土一 | 6a 3b 1a

SO – element; beginning; **SU** – naked, uncovered, simple

素質	soshitsu	nature, makeup	176
質素	shisso	simple, plain	176
元素	genso	chemical element	137
水素	suiso	hydrogen •	21
素人	shirōto	amateur, layman	1

272 一衤 | 1a2 5e

HYŌ – table, chart; surface; expression; **omote** – surface, obverse; **arawa(reru)** – be expressed; **arawa(su)** – express

時間表	jikanhyō	timetable, schedule	42, 43
代表的	daihyōteki	representative, typical	256, 210
表情	hyōjō	facial expression	209
発表	happyō	announcement, publication	96

273 亠衤日 | 2j 5e 4c

RI, ura – reverse side, back, rear

表裏	hyōri	inside and outside; double-dealing	272
裏口	uraguchi	back door, rear entrance	54
裏道	uramichi	back street; secret path	149
裏付け	urazuke	backing, support; corroboration	192
裏切る	uragiru	betray, double-cross	39

274 口一｜ | 3s 1a3 1b2

MEN – face, mask, surface, aspect; **omote, omo, tsura** – face

方面	hōmen	direction, side	70
表面	hyōmen	surface, exterior	272
面会	menkai	interview, meeting	158
面目	menmoku, menboku	face, honor, dignity	55

275	⊢ 一 | 2m 1a2 1b	***SEI, SHŌ, tada(shii)*** – correct, just; ***tada(su)*** – correct; ***masa (ni)*** – just, exactly; certainly

校 正	*kōsei*	proofreading	115
不 正	*fusei*	injustice	94
正 面	*shōmen*	front, front side	274
正 月	*shōgatsu*	January; New Year	17

正　正　正

正　正　正

276	頁口 ゛ 9a 3d 2o	***TŌ, [TO], ZU, atama, kashira*** – head, leader, top

後 頭 (部)	*kōtō(bu)*	back of the head	48, 86
出 頭	*shuttō*	appearance, attendance, presence (at official proceeding)	53
先 頭	*sentō*	(in the) front, lead	50
口 頭	*kōtō*	oral, verbal	54
頭 上	*zujō*	overhead	32

頭　頭　頭

頭　頭　頭

277	頁立 彡 9a 5b 3j	***GAN, kao*** – face

顔 面	*ganmen*	face	274
顔 色	*kaoiro*	complexion; a look	204
素 顔	*sugao*	face without makeup	271
新 顔	*shingao*	stranger; newcomer	174
知 ら ん 顔	*shirankao*	pretend not to notice, ignore	214

顔　顔　顔

顔　顔　顔

278	立 土 一 5b 3b 1a	***SAN*** – childbirth; production; property; ***u(mu)*** – give birth/rise to; ***u(mareru)*** – be born; ***ubu*** – birth; infant

出 産	*shussan*	childbirth, delivery	53
生 産	*seisan*	production	44
産 物	*sanbutsu*	product	79
不 動 産	*fudōsan*	immovable property, real estate	94, 231

産　産　産

産　産　産

279	⺍ 木 一 2o 4a 1a3	**GYŌ** – occupation, business, undertaking; **GŌ** – karma; **waza** – act, deed, work, art

工 業	kōgyō	industry	139
産 業	sangyō	industry	278
事 業	jigyō	undertaking, enterprise	80
実 業 家	jitsugyōka	businessman, industrialist	203, 165

280	犭 3g	**KEN, inu** – dog

番 犬	banken	watchdog	185
愛 犬	aiken	pet/favorite dog	259
野 犬	yaken	stray dog	236
小 犬	koinu	puppy	27
犬 小 屋	inugoya	doghouse	27, 167

281	牛 4g	**GYŪ, ushi** – cow, bull, cattle

牛 肉	gyūniku	beef	223
野 牛	yagyū	buffalo, bison	236
水 牛	suigyū	water buffalo	21
小/子 牛	koushi	calf	27, 103
牛 小 屋	ushigoya	cowshed, barn	27, 167

282	牛 土 十 4g 3b 2k	**TOKU** – special

特 別	tokubetsu	special	267
特 色	tokushoku	distinguishing characteristic	204
特 有	tokuyū	characteristic, peculiar (to)	265
独 特	dokutoku	peculiar, original, unique	219
特 長	tokuchō	strong point, forte	95

283	馬 10a	**BA, uma, [ma]** – horse		
		馬車	*basha*	horse-drawn carriage	133
		馬力	*bariki*	horsepower	100
		馬術	*bajutsu*	horseback riding, dressage	187
		竹馬	*takeuma, chikuba*	stilts	129
		馬小屋	*umagoya*	a stable	27, 167

284	馬尸、 10a 3r 1d	**EKI** – (train) station		
		東京駅	*Tōkyō-eki*	Tokyo Station	71, 189
		当駅	*tōeki*	this station	77
		駅前	*ekimae*	(in) front of/opposite the station	47
		駅長	*ekichō*	stationmaster	95
		駅員	*ekiin*	station employee	163

285	鳥 11b	**CHŌ, tori** – bird		
		白鳥	*hakuchō*	swan	205
		野鳥	*yachō*	wild bird	236
		花鳥	*kachō*	flowers and birds	255
		一石二鳥	*isseki-nichō*	killing 2 birds with 1 stone	2, 78, 3
		鳥居	*torii*	Shinto shrine archway	171

286	山日一 3o 4c 1a2	**TŌ, shima** – island		
		半島	*hantō*	peninsula	88
		島民	*tōmin*	islander	177
		無人島	*mujintō*	uninhabited island	93, 1
		島国	*shimaguni*	island country	40
		島々	*shimajima*	(many) islands	

287	一 丨 ノ 1a2 1b 1c	**MŌ, ke** – hair, fur, feather, down		
		原毛	genmō	raw wool	136
		毛筆	mōhitsu	brush (for writing/painting)	130
		不毛	fumō	barren, sterile	94
		毛糸	keito	wool yarn, knitting wool	242
		まゆ毛	mayuge	eyebrow	

288	゛王 2o 4f	**YŌ, hitsuji** – sheep		
		羊毛	yōmō	wool	287
		羊肉	yōniku	mutton	223
		小/子羊	kohitsuji	lamb	27, 103

289	氵王 ゛ 3a 4f 2o	**YŌ** – ocean; foreign, Western		
		大洋	taiyō	ocean	26
		東洋	tōyō	the East, Orient	71
		西洋	seiyō	the West, Occident	72
		大西洋	Taiseiyō	Atlantic Ocean	26, 72
		洋書	yōsho	foreign/Western book	131

290	魚 11a	**GYO, sakana, uo** – fish		
		魚類	gyorui	a variety of fish	226
		金魚	kingyo	goldfish	23
		魚肉	gyoniku	fish (meat)	223
		魚市場	uoichiba	fish market	181, 154
		魚屋	sakanaya	fish shop/dealer	167

291

｀ 王 戈
2o 4f 4n

義

GI – justice, honor; meaning; in-law; artificial

民主主義	minshu shugi	democracy	177, 155
義務	gimu	obligation, duty	235
義理	giri	duty, debt of gratitude	143
同義語	dōgigo	synonym	198, 67
類義語	ruigigo	word of similar meaning, synonym	226, 67

292

言 王 戈
7a 4f 4n

議

GI – deliberation; proposal

会議	kaigi	conference, meeting	158
協議	kyōgi	council, conference	234
議会	gikai	parliament, diet, congress	158
議員	giin	M.P., dietman, congressman	163
不思議	fushigi	marvel, wonder, mystery	94, 99

293

言 艹 亻
7a 3k 2a

論

RON – discussion, argument; thesis, dissertation

論理	ronri	logic	143
理論	riron	theory	143
世論	yoron, seron	public opinion	252
論議	rongi	discussion, argument	292
論文	ronbun	thesis, essay	111

294

王
4f

王

Ō – king

王国	ōkoku	kingdom	40
国王	kokuō	king	40
女王	joō	queen	102
王子	ōji	prince	103
法王	hōō	pope	123

295	玉 丶 4f 1d	**GYOKU, tama** – gem, jewel; sphere, ball		
		玉石	*gyokuseki*	wheat and chaff, good and bad	78
		玉子	*tamago*	egg (cf. No. 1058)	103
		水玉	*mizutama*	drop of water	21
		目玉	*medama*	eyeball	55
		十円玉	*jūendama*	10-yen piece/coin	12, 13

玉　玉　玉

玉　玉　玉

296	宀玉 丶 3m 4f 1d	**HŌ, takara** – treasure		
		宝石	*hōseki*	precious stone, gem	78
		宝玉	*hōgyoku*	precious stone, gem	295
		国宝	*kokuhō*	national treasure	40
		家宝	*kahō*	family heirloom	165
		宝物	*hōmotsu, takaramono*	treasure, prized possession	79

宝　宝　宝

宝　宝　宝

297	王日ノ 4f 4c 1c	**KŌ, Ō** – emperor		
		天皇	*tennō*	emperor	141
		皇女	*kōjo*	imperial princess	102
		皇居	*kōkyo*	imperial palace	171
		皇室	*kōshitsu*	imperial household	166
		皇位	*kōi*	imperial throne	122

皇　皇　皇

皇　皇　皇

298	王目 丷 4f 5c 2o	**GEN** – present; *arawa(reru)* – appear; *arawa(su)* – show		
		現代	*gendai*	contemporary, modern	256
		現在	*genzai*	current, present; present tense	268
		現金	*genkin*	cash	23
		表現	*hyōgen*	an expression	272
		実現	*jitsugen*	realize, attain; come true	203

現　現　現

現　現　現

299	糸 日 氵				
	6a 4c 3a				

SEN – line

光線	kōsen	light, light ray	138
内線	naisen	(telephone) extension	84
無線	musen	wireless, radio	93
二番線	nibansen	Track No. 2	3, 185
地平線	chiheisen	horizon	118, 202

線 線 線

線 線 線

300	⌢ 日 十				
	3n 4c 2k				

TAN – single, simple

単語	tango	word	67
単位	tan'i	unit, denomination	122
単一	tan'itsu	single, simple, individual	2
単数	tansū	singular (in grammar)	225
単独	tandoku	independent, single-handed	219

単 単 単

単 単 単

301	戈 日 ⌢				
	4n 4c 3n				

SEN, tataka(u) – wage war, fight; **ikusa** – war, battle

内戦	naisen	civil war	84
交戦	kōsen	war, warface	114
合戦	kassen	battle; contest	159
休戦	kyūsen	truce, cease-fire	60
戦後	sengo	postwar	48

戦 戦 戦

戦 戦 戦

302	ク 十 一				
	2n 2k 1a2				

SŌ, araso(u) – dispute, argue, contend for

戦争	sensō	war	301
争議	sōgi	dispute, strife	292
論争	ronsō	argument, controversy	293
争点	sōten	point of contention, issue	169
言い争う	iiarasou	quarrel, argue	66

争 争 争

争 争 争

303

ク 心 一
2n 4k 1a3

KYŪ – urgent, sudden; **iso(gu)** – be in a hurry

急行	kyūkō	an express (train)	68
特急	tokkyū	a special express (train)	282
急変	kyūhen	sudden change	257
急用	kyūyō	urgent business	107
急性	kyūsei	acute	98

304

心 口 一
4k 3s 1a2

AKU, O, waru(i) – bad, evil

悪化	akka	change for the worse	254
悪性	akusei	malignant, vicious	98
悪事	akuji	evil deed	80
最悪	saiaku	the worst, at worst	263
悪口	akkō, warukuchi	abusive language, speaking ill of	54

305

一 木
1a 4a

MATSU, BATSU, sue – end

週末	shūmatsu	weekend	91
月末	getsumatsu	end of the month	17
年末	nenmatsu	year's end	45
末代	matsudai	all ages to come, eternity	256
末っ子	suekko	youngest child	103

306

一 木
1a 4a

MI – not yet

未来	mirai	future	69
未知	michi	unknown	214
前代未聞	zendaimimon	unprecedented	47, 256, 64
未満	miman	less than, under	201
未明	mimei	early dawn, before daybreak	18

307

口 木 一
3d 4a 1a

味

MI, aji – taste; ***aji(wau)*** – taste; relish, appreciate

意味	imi	meaning, significance, sense	132
正味	shōmi	net (amount/weight/price)	275
不気味	bukimi	uncanny, eerie, ominous	94, 134
地味	jimi	plain, subdued, undemonstrative	118
三味線	shamisen	samisen (3-stringed instrument)	4, 299

308

ネ 土
4e 3b

社

SHA – Shinto shrine; company, firm; ***yashiro*** – Shinto shrine

社会	shakai	society, social	158
会社	kaisha	company, firm	158
本社	honsha	our company; head office	25
社長	shachō	company president	95
社員	shain	employee, staff member	163

309

| 日
1b 4c

申

SHIN, mō(su) – say; be named

答申	tōshin	report, findings	160
上申	jōshin	report (to a superior)	32
内申	naishin	unofficial/confidential report	84
申し入れ	mōshiire	offer, proposal, notice	52
申し合わせ	mōshiawase	an understanding	159

310

ネ 日 |
4e 4c 1b

神

SHIN, JIN, kami, [kan], [kō] – god, God

神道	shintō	Shintoism	149
神社	jinja	Shinto shrine	308
神話	shinwa	myth, mythology	238
神父	shinpu	(Catholic) priest, Father	113
神風	kamikaze	divine wind; kamikaze	29

311	一 亻 ノ 1a2 2a 1c

SHITSU, ushina(u) – lose

失業	shitsugyō	unemployment	279
失意	shitsui	disappointment, despair	132
失神	shisshin	faint, lose consciousness	310
失恋	shitsuren	unrequited love	258
見失う	miushinau	lose sight of	63

312	金 亻 一 8a 2a 1a2

TETSU – iron

鉄道	tetsudō	railroad	149
地下鉄	chikatetsu	subway	118, 31
私鉄	shitetsu	private railway	125
鉄かぶと	tetsukabuto	steel helmet	

313	金 日 ノ 8a 4c 1c

GIN – silver

銀行	ginkō	bank	68
日銀	Nichigin	the Bank of Japan	5
銀色	gin'iro	silver color	204
水銀	suigin	mercury	21
銀メダル	ginmedaru	silver medal	

314	木 日 ノ 4a 4c 1c

KON – root; perseverance; **ne** – root, base, origin

大根	daikon	daikon, Japanese radish	26
根本的	konponteki	fundamental; radical	25, 210
根気	konki	patience, perseverance	134
屋根	yane	roof	167
根強い	nezuyoi	deep-rooted, firmly established	217

315	一 亻 1a2 2a	**FU, [FŪ], otto** – husband, man			
		夫 人	*fujin*	wife, Mrs.	1
		人 夫	*ninpu*	laborer	1
		水 夫	*suifu*	sailor, seaman	21
		工 夫	*kōfu*	laborer	139
			kufū	contrivance, scheme, means	

夫

316	女 巾 一 3e 3f 2i	**FU** – woman, wife			
		夫 婦	*fūfu*	husband and wife, married couple	315
		主 婦	*shufu*	housewife	155
		婦 人	*fujin*	lady, woman	1
		婦 女 (子)	*fujo(shi)*	woman	102, 103
		婦 長	*fuchō*	head nurse	95

婦

317	刂 巾 一 2f 3f 2i	**KI, kae(ru)** – return; **kae(su)** – let return, dismiss			
		帰 国	*kikoku*	return to one's country	40
		帰 宅	*kitaku*	return/come/get home	178
		帰 路	*kiro*	the way home	151
		帰 化	*kika*	become naturalized	254
		日 帰 り	*higaeri*	go and return in a day	5

帰

318	十 又 2k 2h	**SHI** – branch; support; **sasa(eru)** – support			
		支 出	*shishutsu*	expenditure, disbursement	53
		支 社	*shisha*	branch (office)	308
		支 店	*shiten*	branch office/store	168
		支 部	*shibu*	branch, local chapter	86
		支 流	*shiryū*	tributary (of a river)	247

支

319 米 十 、
6b 2k 1d2

料

RYŌ – materials; fee

料理	ryōri	cooking, cuisine; dish, food	143
原料	genryō	raw materials	136
料金	ryōkin	fee, charge, fare	23
手数料	tesūryō	fee; commission	57, 225
有/無料	yū/muryō	pay, toll, charging a fee/free	265, 93

320 禾 十 、
5d 2k 1d2

科

KA – academic course, department, faculty

科学	kagaku	science	109
理科	rika	natural science (department)	143
外科	geka	surgery	93
産婦人科医	sanfujinkai	gynecologist	278, 316, 1, 220
教科書	kyōkasho	textbook, schoolbook	245, 131

321 一 日 丨
(1a) 4c 1b

良

RYŌ, yo(i) – good

良好	ryōkō	good, favorable, satisfactory	104
良質	ryōshitsu	good quality	176
最良	sairyō	best	263
不良	furyō	bad, unsatisfactory; delinquency	94
良心	ryōshin	conscience	97

322 食
8b

食

SHOKU, [JIKI] – food; eating; **ta(beru), ku(u/rau)** – eat

食事	shokuji	meal, dinner	80
食料品	shokuryōhin	food, foodstuffs	319, 230
和/洋食	wa/yō-shoku	Japanese/Western food	124, 289
夕食	yūshoku	evening meal, supper	81
食べ物	tabemono	food	79

323	食 欠 8b 4j

IN, no(mu) – drink

飲食	inshoku	food and drink, eating and drinking	322
飲料	inryō	drink, beverage	319
飲料水	inryōsui	drinking water	319, 21
飲み水	nomimizu	drinking water	21
飲み物	nomimono	(something to) drink, beverage	79

324	厂 又 2p 2h

HAN, [HON] – anti-; **[TAN]** – (unit of land/cloth measurement); **so(ru/rasu)** – (intr./tr.) warp, bend back

反発	hanpatsu	repulsion, repellence; opposition	96
反日	han-Nichi	anti-Japanese	5
反面	hanmen	the other side	274
反省	hansei	reflection, introspection; reconsideration	145

325	食 厂 又 8b 2p 2h

HAN, meshi – cooked rice; meal, food

ご飯	gohan	cooked rice; meal, food	
赤飯	sekihan	(festive) rice boiled with red beans	207
夕飯	yūhan, yūmeshi	evening meal, supper, dinner	81
飯ごう	hangō	mess kit, eating utensils	
飯場	hanba	construction camp/bunkhouse	154

326	宀 口 3m 3d2

KAN – government, authorities

半官半民	hankan-hanmin	semigovernmental	88, 177
国務長官	kokumu chōkan	secretary of state	40, 235, 95
外交官	gaikōkan	diplomat	83, 114
高官	kōkan	high government official/office	190
神官	shinkan	Shinto priest	310

327	食 宀 口
	8b 3m 3d2

KAN – (large) building, hall

旅館	ryokan	Japanese-style inn	222
水族館	suizokukan	aquarium	22, 221
会館	kaikan	(assembly) hall	158
本館	honkan	main building	25
別館	bekkan	annex, extension	267

館

328	竹 宀 口
	6f 3m 3d2

KAN – pipe; wind instrument; control; **kuda** – pipe, tube

管内	kannai	(area of) jurisdiction	84
管理	kanri	administration, supervision	143
水道管	suidōkan	water pipe/conduit	21, 149
気管	kikan	windpipe, trachea	134
鉄管	tekkan	iron tube/pipe	312

管

329	禾 刂
	5d 2f

RI – advantage; (loan) interest; **ki(ku)** – take effect, work

有利	yūri	profitable, advantageous	265
利子	rishi	interest (on a loan)	103
利用	riyō	make use of	107
利口	rikō	smart, clever, bright	54
左利き	hidarikiki	left-hander	75

利

330	亻 日 一
	2a 4c 1a

BEN – convenience; excrement; **BIN** – opportunity; mail; **tayo(ri)** – news, tidings

便利	benri	convenient, handy	329
不便	fuben	inconvenient	94
便所	benjo	toilet	153
別便	betsubin	separate mail	267

便

331	イ口一 2a 3s 1a	**SHI** – use; messenger; *tsuka(u)* – use		
		大使	*taishi*	ambassador	26
		公使	*kōshi*	minister, envoy	126
		天使	*tenshi*	angel	141
		使用法	*shiyōhō*	how to use, directions for use	107, 123
		使い方	*tsukaikata*	how to use, way to handle	70

332	一口丨 (1a) 3s 1b	**SHI** – history, chronicles		
		日本史	*nihonshi*	Japanese history	5, 25
		中世史	*chūseishi*	medieval history	28, 252
		文学史	*bungakushi*	history of literature	111, 109
		史実	*shijitsu*	historical fact	203
		女史	*joshi*	(honorific) Madame, Miss, Mrs.	102

333	イ士 2a 3p	**SHI, [JI]**, *tsuka(eru)* – serve		
		仕事	*shigoto*	work, job	80
		仕立て屋	*shitateya*	tailor; dressmaker	121, 167
		仕方	*shikata*	way, method, means	70
		仕手	*shite*	protagonist, leading role (in Noh)	57
		仕上げる	*shiageru*	finish up, complete	32

334	イ士ノ 2a 3p 1c	**NIN** – duty, responsibility, office; *maka(seru/su)* – entrust (to)		
		主任	*shunin*	person in charge, manager, head	155
		信任	*shinnin*	confidence, trust	157
		後任	*kōnin*	successor	48
		任務	*ninmu*	duty, office, mission	235
		任意	*nin'i*	optional, voluntary	132

335	木 4a	隹 8c	一 1a2	**KEN, [GON]** – authority, power; right		
				権利	kenri	a right	329
				人権	jinken	human rights	1
				特権	tokken	special right, privilege	282
				主権	shuken	sovereignty	155
				三権分立	sanken bunritsu	separation of powers	4, 38, 121

336	木 4a	口 3d	又 2h	**KYOKU** – end, pole; **GOKU** – very, extremely; *kiwa(mi)* – height, end; *kiwa(meru/ maru)* – carry to/reach its end		
				北/南極	hok/nan-kyoku	north/south pole	73, 74
				極東	kyokutō	the Far East	71
				極上	gokujō	finest, top quality	32
				見極める	mikiwameru	see through, discern	63

337	口 3d	一 1a	ノ 1c	**KU** – phrase, sentence, verse		
				語句	goku	words and phrases	67
				成句	seiku	set phrase, idiom	261
				文句	monku	words, expression; objection	111
				句読点	kutōten	punctuation mark	244, 169
				引用句	in'yōku	quotation	216, 107

338	日 4c	一 1a	ノ 1c	**JUN** – 10-day period		
				上旬	jōjun	first 10 days of a month (1st to 10th)	32
				中旬	chūjun	second 10 days of a month (11th to 20th)	28
				下旬	gejun	last third of a month (21st to end)	31

339	口 ノ 、 3s 1c 1d3	**ZU** – drawing, diagram, plan; **TO, haka(ru)** – plan

図

地 図	chizu	map	118
図 表	zuhyō	chart, table, graph	272
合 図	aizu	signal, sign, gesture	159
意 図	ito	intention	132
図 書 館	toshokan	library	131, 327

340	言 十 7a 2k	**KEI** – measuring; plan; total; **haka(ru)** – measure, compute; **haka(rau)** – arrange, dispose of, see about

計

時 計	tokei	clock, watch	42
会 計	kaikei	accounting; paying a bill	158
合 計	gōkei	total	159
家 計	kakei	household finances	165

341	金 十 8a 2k	**SHIN, hari** – needle

針

方 針	hōshin	course, line, policy	70
針 路	shinro	course (of a ship)	151
長/分 針	chō/funshin	minute hand	95, 38
短 針	tanshin	hour hand	215
針 金	harigane	wire	23

342	言 土 口 7a 3b 3d	**CHŌ, shira(beru)** – investigate, check; **totono(eru)** – prepare, arrange, put in order; **totono(u)** – be prepared, arranged

調

強 調	kyōchō	cooperation, harmony	234
好 調	kōchō	good, favorable	104
調 子	chōshi	tone; mood; condition	103
取 り 調 べ	torishirabe	investigation, questioning	65

343	一 日 l 1a 4c 1b3	**GA** – picture; **KAKU** – stroke (in writing kanji)		
		画家 *gaka* painter		165
		日本/洋画 *nihon/yō-ga* Japanese/Western-style painting		5, 25, 289
		画用紙 *gayōshi* drawing paper		107, 180
		画面 *gamen* (TV/movie/computer) screen		274
		計画 *keikaku* plan, project		340

344	氵 日 宀 3a 4c 3m	**EN** – performance, presentation, play		
		上演 *jōen* performance, dramatic presentation		32
		公演 *kōen* public performance		126
		独演 *dokuen* solo performance		219
		出演 *shutsuen* appearance, performance		53
		演出 *enshutsu* production, staging (of a play)		53

345	糸 亻 一 6a 2a 1a2	**KAI, E** – picture		
		絵画 *kaiga* pictures, paintings, drawings		343
		絵葉書 *ehagaki* picture postcard		253, 131
		絵本 *ehon* picture book		25
		口絵 *kuchie* frontispiece		54
		大和絵 *Yamato-e* ancient Japanese-style painting		26, 124

346	糸 口 亻 6a 3d 2a	**KYŪ** – supply		
		給料 *kyūryō* pay, wages, salary		319
		月給 *gekkyū* monthly salary		17
		支給 *shikyū* supply, provisioning, allowance		318
		供給 *kyōkyū* supply		197
		給水 *kyūsui* water supply		21

347	立 日 5b 4c	**ON, IN, oto, ne** – sound			
		発音	*hatsuon*	pronunciation	96
		表音文字	*hyōon moji*	phonetic symbol	272, 111, 110
		母音	*boin*	vowel	112
		本音	*honne*	one's true intention	25
		足音	*ashioto*	sound of footsteps	58

音

348	日 立 4c2 5b	**AN, kura(i)** – dark, dim			
		暗黒	*ankoku*	darkness	206
		暗室	*anshitsu*	darkroom	166
		暗号	*angō*	(secret) code, cipher	266
		明暗	*meian*	light and darkness, shading	18
		暗がり	*kuragari*	darkness	

暗

349	貝 立 日 7b 5b 4c	**IN** – rhyme			
		音韻学	*on'ingaku*	phonology	347, 109
		韻文	*inbun*	verse, poetry	111
		韻語	*ingo*	rhyming words	67
		頭韻	*tōin*	alliteration	276

韻

350	扌 貝 口 3c 7b 3d	**SON** – loss, damage; **soko(nau/neru)** – harm, injure; **-soko(nau)** – fail to, err in			
		損失	*sonshitsu*	loss	311
		大損	*ōzon*	great loss	26
		見損なう	*misokonau*	miss (seeing); misjudge	63
		読み損なう	*yomisokonau*	misread	244

損

351	一 冂 イ (1a) 2r 2a	**Ō** – center, middle		
		中央	*chūō*	center	28
		中央口	*chūōguchi*	main/middle exit	28, 54
		中央部	*chūōbu*	central part, middle	28, 86
		中央線	*Chūō-sen*	the Chuo (train) Line	28, 299
		中央区	*Chūō-ku*	Chuo Ward (Tokyo)	28, 183

央　央　央

央　央　央

352	日 冂 イ 4c 2r 2a	**EI, utsu(su)** – reflect, project; **utsu(ru)** – be reflected, projected; **ha(eru)** – shine, be brilliant		
		映画	*eiga*	movie	343
		反映	*han'ei*	reflection	324
		上映	*jōei*	showing, screening (of a movie)	32
		夕映え	*yūbae*	the glow of sunset	81

映　映　映

映　映　映

353	艹 冂 イ 3k 2r 2a	**EI** – brilliant, talented, gifted		
		英気	*eiki*	energetic spirit, enthusiasm	134
		石英	*sekiei*	quartz	78
		英語	*Eigo*	the English language	67
		和英	*Wa-Ei*	Japanese-English	124
		英会話	*Eikaiwa*	English conversation	158, 238

英　英　英

英　英　英

354	頁 日 卜 9a 4c 2m	**DAI** – topic, theme; title		
		問題	*mondai*	problem, question	162
		議題	*gidai*	topic for discussion, agenda	292
		話題	*wadai*	topic	238
		表題	*hyōdai*	title, caption	272
		宿題	*shukudai*	homework	179

題　題　題

題　題　題

355	宀 卜 亻 3m 2m 2a	**TEI, JŌ, sada(meru)** – determine, decide; **sada(maru)** – be determined, decided; **sada(ka)** – certain, definite

安定	*antei*	stability, equilibrium	105
協定	*kyōtei*	agreement, pact	234
定食	*teishoku*	meal of fixed menu, complete meal	322
未定	*mitei*	undecided, unsettled, not yet fixed	306

356	氵 亻 一 3a 2a 1a2	**KETSU, ki(meru)** – decide; **ki(maru)** – be decided

決定	*kettei*	decision, determination	355
決心	*kesshin*	determination, resolution	97
決意	*ketsui*	determination, resolution	132
議決	*giketsu*	decision (of a committee)	292
未決	*miketsu*	pending	306

357	氵 王 丶 3a 4f 1d	**CHŪ** – note, comment; **soso(gu)** – pour, flow

注意	*chūi*	attention, caution, warning	132
注目	*chūmoku*	attention, notice	55
注文	*chūmon*	order, commission	111
発注	*hatchū*	order, commission	96
注入	*chūnyū*	injection; pour into, infuse	52

358	艹 日 氵 4a 4c 2b	**GAKU** – music; **RAKU** – pleasure; **tano(shimu)** – enjoy; **tano(shii)** – fun, enjoyable, pleasant

音楽	*ongaku*	music	347
文楽	*bunraku*	Japanese puppet theater	111
楽天家	*rakutenka*	optimist	141, 165
安楽死	*anrakushi*	euthanasia	105, 85

359	艹 日 木 3k 4c 4a	**YAKU, kusuri** – medicine		
		薬学	*yakugaku*	pharmacy	109
		薬品	*yakuhin*	medicines, drugs	230
		薬味	*yakumi*	spices	307
		薬局	*yakkyoku*	pharmacy	170
		薬屋	*kusuriya*	drugstore, pharmacy	167

360	亻 ト 一 2a 2m 1a2	**SAKU, SA, tsuku(ru)** – make		
		作家	*sakka*	writer	165
		作品	*sakuhin*	(literary) work, work (of art), opus	230
		作戦	*sakusen*	military operation, tactics	301
		作り話	*tsukuribanashi*	made-up story, fabrication	238
		手作り	*tezukuri*	handmade	57

361	日 ト 一 4c 2m 1a2	**SAKU** – past, yesterday		
		昨年	*sakunen*	last year	45
		昨日	*sakujitsu, kinō*	yesterday	5
		一昨日	*issakujitsu, ototoi*	day before yesterday	2, 5
		一昨年	*issakunen, ototoshi*	year before last	2, 45
		昨今	*sakkon*	these days, recent	51

362	几 又 ト 2s 2h 2m	**DAN** – step; stairs; rank; column		
		一段	*ichidan*	step; single-stage	2
		石段	*ishidan*	stone stairway	78
		段々畑	*dandanbatake*	terraced fields	36
		手段	*shudan*	means, measure	57
		段取り	*dandori*	program, plan, arrangements	65

363	一 日 l	*YU, YŪ, [YUI], yoshi* – reason, cause; significance		
	(1a) 4c 1b	由来	*yurai*	origin, derivation	69
		理由	*riyū*	reason, grounds	143
		自由	*jiyū*	freedom	62
		不自由	*fujiyū*	discomfort; want, privation	94, 62
		事由	*jiyū*	reason, cause	80

由

364	氵 日 l	*YU, abura* – oil		
	3a 4c 1b	石油	*sekiyu*	oil, petroleum	78
		原油	*gen'yu*	crude oil	136
		油田	*yuden*	oil field	35
		給油所	*kyūyusho, kyūyujo*	filling/gas station	346, 153
		油絵	*aburae*	oil painting	345

油

365	亠 十 ノ	*TAI* – against; *TSUI* – pair		
	2j 2k 1c	反対	*hantai*	opposite; opposition	324
		対立	*tairitsu*	confrontation	121
		対決	*taiketsu*	showdown	356
		対面	*taimen*	interview, meeting	274
		対話	*taiwa*	conversation, dialogue	238

対

366	一 日 l	*KYOKU* – curve; melody, musical composition; *ma(geru)* – bend, distort; *ma(garu)* – (intr.) bend, turn		
	(1a) 4c 1b2	作曲	*sakkyoku*	musical composition	360
		名曲	*meikyoku*	famous/well-known melody	82
		曲線	*kyokusen*	a curve	299
		曲がり道	*magarimichi*	winding street	149

曲

367	⺮ ⺍ 冂 2o 3k 2r	**_TEN_** – law code; ceremony		
		古典	_koten_	classical literature, the classics	172
		百科事典	_hyakkajiten_	encyclopedia	14, 320, 80
		法典	_hōten_	code of laws	123
		出典	_shutten_	literary source, authority	53
		特典	_tokuten_	special favor, privilege	282

典

368	⺍ 口 冂 2o 3d 2r	**_KŌ, KYŌ_** – interest; entertainment; liveliness; prosperity; **_oko(ru)_** – flourish, prosper; **_oko(su)_** – revive, retrieve		
		興行	_kōgyō_	entertainment industry; performance	68
		興信所	_kōshinjo_	private inquiry/detective agency	157, 153
		興業	_kōgyō_	industrial enterprise	279
		興味	_kyōmi_	interest	307

興

369	厂 日 一 2p 4c 1a2	**_NŌ_** – agriculture		
		農業	_nōgyō_	agriculture	279
		農村	_nōson_	farm village	191
		農民	_nōmin_	farmer, peasant	177
		農家	_nōka_	farmhouse, farm household; farmer	165
		農産物	_nōsanbutsu_	agricultural product	278, 79

農

370	一 丨 1a2 1b	**_KO, KI, onore_** – self		
		自己	_jiko_	self-	62
		自己中心	_jiko chūshin_	egocentric	62, 28, 97
		利己	_riko_	selfishness, egoism	329
		利己的	_rikoteki_	selfish, self-centered	329, 210
		知己	_chiki_	acquaintance	214

己

371	言 一 丨
	7a 1a2 1b

KI, shiru(su) – write/note down

記者	kisha	newspaperman, journalist	164
記事	kiji	article, report	80
日記	nikki	diary	5
暗記	anki	memorize	348
記号	kigō	mark, symbol	266

372	糸 一 丨
	6a 1a2 1b

KI – narrative, history

紀元	kigen	era (of year reckoning)	137
紀元前/後	kigen-zen/go	B.C./A.D.	137, 47, 48
世紀	seiki	century	252
紀行 (文)	kikō(bun)	account of a journey	68, 111
風紀	fūki	discipline, public morals	29

373	土 卜 亻
	3b 2m 2a

KI – awakening, rise, beginning; **o(kiru)** – get/wake/be up; **o(koru)** – occur; **o(kosu)** – give rise; wake (someone) up

起原	kigen	origin, beginning	136
起点	kiten	starting point	169
早起き	hayaoki	get up early	248
起き上がる	okiagaru	get up, pick oneself up	32

374	亻 日 十
	3i 4c 2k

TOKU – profit, advantage; **e(ru), u(ru)** – gain, acquire

損得	sontoku	profit and loss	350
所得	shotoku	income	153
得点	tokuten	one's score, points made	169
得意	tokui	prosperity; pride; one's strong point	132
心得る	kokoroeru	know, understand	97

375	彳 几 又 3i 2s 2h	**YAKU** – service, use; office, post; **EKI** – battle; service	
		役所　　　yakusho　　　government office/bureau	153
		役人　　　yakunin　　　public official	1
		役員　　　yakuin　　　(company) officer, director	163
		役者　　　yakusha　　　player, actor	164
		使役　　　shieki　　　employment, service	331

役

376	舟 口 丶丶 6c 3d 2o	**SEN, fune, [funa]** – ship	
		船長　　　senchō　　　captain	95
		船員　　　sen'in　　　crewman, seaman, sailor	163
		船室　　　senshitsu　　　cabin	166
		汽船　　　kisen　　　steamship, steamer	135
		船旅　　　funatabi　　　sea voyage	222

船

377	广 艹 又 3q 3k 2h	**DO, [TAKU], [TO]** – degree, measure, limit; times; **tabi** – times	
		一度　　　　ichido　　　once; 1 degree (of temperature/arc)	2
		今度　　　　kondo　　　this time; soon; next time	51
		年度　　　　nendo　　　business/fiscal year	45
		高度成長　　kōdo seichō　　high growth	190, 261, 95
		支/仕度　　　shitaku　　　preparations	318, 333

度

378	氵 厂 艹 3a 2p 3k	**TO, wata(ru)** – cross; **wata(su)** – hand over	
		渡来　　　torai　　　introduction (into); visit	69
		渡し船　　watashibune　　ferryboat	376
		渡り鳥　　wataridori　　migratory bird	285
		見渡す　　miwatasu　　look out over	63
		手渡す　　tewatasu　　hand deliver, hand over	57

渡

379	广 艹 巾 3q 3k 3f

SEKI – seat, place

出席	shusseki	attendance	53
満席	manseki	full, fully occupied	201
議席	giseki	seat (in parliament)	292
主席	shuseki	top seat, head, chief	155
席上	sekijō	(at) the meeting; (on) the occasion	32

席

380	疒 门 亻 5i 2r 2a

BYŌ, [HEI], ya(mu) – fall ill, suffer from; **yamai** – illness

病気	byōki	sickness, disease	134
重病	jūbyō	serious illness	227
急病	kyūbyō	sudden illness	303
性病	seibyō	venereal disease	98
病人	byōnin	sick person	1

病

381	心 立 日 4k2 5b 4c

OKU – remember, think

| 記憶 | kioku | memory, recollection | 371 |
| 憶病 | okubyō | cowardice, timidity | 380 |

憶

382	亻 立 日 2a 5b 4c

OKU – 100 million

一億	ichioku	100 million	2
億万長者	okuman chōja	multimillionaire	16, 95, 164
数億年	sūokunen	hundreds of millions of years	225, 45

億

383 欠 4j	**KETSU**, *ka(ku)* – lack; *ka(keru)* – be lacking		
	欠点	ketten	defect, flaw	169
	出欠	shukketsu	attendance (and/or absence)	53
	欠席	kesseki	absence, nonattendance	379
	欠員	ketsuin	vacant position, opening	163
	欠損	kesson	deficit, loss	350

384 冫 欠 2b 4j	**JI, SHI**, *tsugi* – next; *tsu(gu)* – come/rank next		
	次官	jikan	vice-minister	326
	次男	jinan	second-oldest son	101
	二次	niji	second, secondary	3
	目次	mokuji	table of contents	55
	相次ぐ	aitsugu	follow/happen one after another	146

385 耳 立 戈 6e 5b 4n	**SHOKU** – employment, job, occupation, office		
	職業	shokugyō	occupation, profession	279
	職場	shokuba	place of work, jobsite	154
	職員	shokuin	personnel, staff, staff member	163
	現職	genshoku	one's present post	298
	無職	mushoku	unemployed	93

386 月 卜 ノ 4b 2m2 1c	**NŌ** – ability, function; Noh play		
	能力	nōryoku	capacity, talent	100
	本能	honnō	instinct	25
	能筆	nōhitsu	calligraphy, skilled penmanship	130
	能楽	nōgaku	Noh play	358
	能面	nōmen	Noh mask	274

387	心 月 卜
	4k 4b 2m2

TAI – condition, appearance

態 度	taido	attitude	377
生 態	seitai	mode of life, ecology	44
変 態	hentai	metamorphosis; abnormality	257
事 態	jitai	situation, state of affairs	80
実 態	jittai	actual conditions/situation	203

態　態　態

態　態　態

388	口 一 丨
	3d 1a 1b

KA – good; possible; approval

可 能 (性)	kanō(sei)	possibility	386, 98
不 可 能	fukanō	impossible	94, 386
不 可 欠	fukaketsu	indispensable, essential	94, 383
不 可 分	fukabun	indivisible	94, 38
可 決	kaketsu	approval (of a proposed law)	356

可　可　可

可　可　可

389	氵 口 一
	3a 3d 1a

KA, kawa – river

河 川	kasen	rivers	33
河 口	kakō, kawaguchi	mouth of a river	54
大 河	taiga	large river	26
銀 河	ginga	the Milky Way	313
河 原	kawara	dry riverbed	136

河　河　河

河　河　河

390	亻 口 一
	2a 3d 1a

KA, nani, [nan] – what, which, how many

何 事	nanigoto	what, whatever	80
何 曜 日	nan(i)yōbi	what day of the week	19, 5
何 日	nannichi	how many days; what day of the month	5
何 時	nanji	what time	42
何 時 間	nanjikan	how many hours	42, 43

何　何　何

何　何　何

391	艹 口 亻 3k 3d 2a	**KA, ni** – load, cargo, baggage	
		在荷 *zaika* stock, inventory	268
		入荷 *nyūka* fresh supply/arrival of goods	52
		出荷 *shukka* shipment, shipping	53
		(手)荷物 *(te)nimotsu* (hand)baggage, luggage	57, 79
		重荷 *omoni* heavy burden	227

荷　荷　荷

荷　荷　荷

392	欠 口 一 4j 3d2 1a2	**KA, uta** – poem, song; **uta(u)** – sing	
		歌手 *kashu* singer	57
		国歌 *kokka* national anthem	40
		和歌 *waka* 31-syllable Japanese poem	124
		短歌 *tanka* (synonym for *waka*)	215
		流行歌 *ryūkōka* popular song	247, 68

歌　歌　歌

歌　歌　歌

393	一 丨 丶 1a2 1b 1d	**YO** – previously, in advance	
		予約 *yoyaku* subscription, reservation, booking	211
		予定 *yotei* plan; expectation	355
		予想 *yosō* expectation, supposition	147
		予知 *yochi* foresee, predict	214
		予言 *yogen* prophecy, prediction	66

予　予　予

予　予　予

394	頁 一 丨 9a 1a2 1b	**YO, azu(keru/karu)** – entrust/receive for safekeeping	
		預金 *yokin* deposit, bank account	23
		預かり所 *azukarisho, azukarijo* depository, warehouse	153
		手荷物一時預かり(所) *tenimotsu ichiji azukari(sho/jo)*	
		(place for) temporary handbaggage storage	
			57, 391, 79, 2, 42, 153

預　預　預

預　預　預

395	彡 艹 一 3j 3k 1a	**KEI, GYŌ, katachi, kata** – form, shape		
		円形	enkei	round/circular shape	13
		正方形	seihōkei	square	275, 70
		無形	mukei	formless, immaterial, intangible	93
		人形	ningyō	doll, puppet	1
		手形	tegata	(bank) bill, note, draft	57

396	門 艹 一 8e 3k 1a	**KAI** – opening, development; **a(ku/keru)** – (intr./tr.) open; **hira(keru)** – become developed; **hira(ku)** – (tr.) open		
		公開	kōkai	open to the public	126
		開会	kaikai	opening of a meeting	158
		未開	mikai	uncivilized, backward, savage	306
		開発	kaihatsu	development	96

397	門 十 ノ 8e 2k 1c	**HEI, shi(meru), to(jiru/zasu)** – close, shut; **shi(maru)** – become closed		
		開閉	kaihei	opening and closing	396
		閉会	heikai	closing, adjournment	158
		閉店	heiten	store closing	168
		閉口	heikō	be dumbfounded	54

398	門 ﹀ 亻 8e 2o 2a	**KAN, seki** – barrier		
		関門	kanmon	gateway, barrier	161
		関心	kanshin	interest	97
		関東	Kantō	(region including Tokyo)	71
		関西	Kansai	(region including Osaka and Kyoto)	72
		関所	sekisho	barrier station, checkpoint	153

399 禾口〵 5d 3d 2o2	**ZEI** – tax		
	税金	zeikin	tax	23
	所得税	shotokuzei	income tax	153, 374
	関税	kanzei	customs, duty, tariff	398
	税関	zeikan	customs, customshouse	398
	無税	muzei	tax-free, duty-free	93

400 言口〵 7a 3d 2o2	**SETSU** – opinion, theory; **ZEI, to(ku)** – explain; persuade		
	説明	setsumei	explanation	18
	社説	shasetsu	an editorial	308
	小説	shōsetsu	novel, story	27
	演説	enzetsu	a speech	344
	説教	sekkyō	sermon	245

401 〵王亻 2o 4f 2a	**BI, utsuku(shii)** – beautiful		
	美術館	bijutsukan	art museum/gallery	187, 327
	美学	bigaku	esthetics	109
	美人	bijin	beautiful woman	1
	美化	bika	beautification	254
	美点	biten	beauty, merit, good point	169

402 〵食王 2o 8b 4f	**YŌ, yashina(u)** – rear; adopt; support; recuperate		
	養育	yōiku	upbringing, nurture	246
	養成	yōsei	training, cultivation	261
	教養	kyōyō	culture, education	245
	養子	yōshi	adopted child	103
	休養	kyūyō	rest, recreation; recuperation	60

403 様
4a 4f 2o

YŌ – way, manner; similarity; condition; *sama* – condition; Mr., Mrs., Miss

様子	*yōsu*	situation, aspect, appearance	103
同様	*dōyō*	same	198
多様	*tayō*	diversity, variety	229
神様	*kamisama*	God	310
田中明様	*Tanaka Akira sama*	Mr. Akira Tanaka	35, 28, 18

404 第
6f 3h 1b

DAI – (prefix for ordinals), degree

第一	*daiichi*	No. 1; first, best, main	2
毎月第二土曜日	*maitsuki daini doyōbi*	second Saturday of every month	116, 17, 3, 24, 19, 5
第三者	*daisansha*	third person/party	4, 164
次第	*shidai*	sequence; circumstances; as soon as	384

405 弟
2o 3h 1b

TEI, [DAI], [DE], otōto – younger brother

義弟	*gitei*	younger brother-in-law	291
子弟	*shitei*	sons, children	103
弟子	*deshi*	pupil, apprentice, disciple	103
門弟	*montei*	pupil, follower	161
弟分	*otōtobun*	like a younger brother	38

406 兄
3d 2o

KEI, [KYŌ], ani – elder brother

兄弟	*kyōdai*	brothers, brothers and sisters	405
父兄	*fukei*	parents and brothers; guardians	113
義兄	*gikei*	elder brother-in-law	291
実兄	*jikkei*	one's brother by blood	203
兄さん	*niisan*	elder brother	

407	女 巾 亠 3e 3f 2j	**SHI, ane** – elder sister

| 義姉 | gishi | elder sister-in-law | 291 |
| 姉さん | nēsan | elder sister; young lady | |

姉

408	女 木 一 3e 4a 1a	**MAI, imōto** – younger sister

姉妹	shimai	sisters	407
姉妹都市	shimai toshi	sister cities	407, 188, 181
弟妹	teimai	younger brothers and sisters	405
義妹	gimai	younger sister-in-law	291

妹

409	巾 口 一 3f 3d2 1a	**SHI** – teacher; army

教師	kyōshi	teacher, instructor	245
医師	ishi	physician	220
法師	hōshi	Buddhist priest	123
山師	yamashi	speculator; adventurer; charlatan	34
師弟	shitei	master and pupil	405

師

410	立 日 土 5b 4c 3b	**DŌ, warabe** – child

学童	gakudō	schoolchild	109
童話	dōwa	nursery story, fairy tale	238
童顔	dōgan	childlike/boyish face	277
童心	dōshin	child's mind/feelings	97
神童	shindō	child prodigy	310

童

411 量 〔日 4c2 土 3b 一 1a〕

RYŌ – quantity; **haka(ru)** – (tr.) measure, weigh

大/小量	tai/shōryō	large/small quantity	26, 144
雨量	uryō	(amount of) rainfall	30
大量生産	tairyō seisan	mass production	26, 44, 278
分量	bunryō	quantity, amount; dosage	38
重量	jūryō	weight	227

412 商 〔亠 2j 口 3d ⺍ 2o2〕

SHŌ, akina(u) – deal (in), trade

商人	shōnin	merchant, dealer	1
商品	shōhin	goods, merchandise	230
商業	shōgyō	commerce, business	279
商売	shōbai	trade, business; one's trade	239
商工	shōkō	commerce and industry	139

413 過 〔辶 2q 口 3d 冂 2r2〕

KA, su(giru) – pass, exceed, too much; **su(gosu)** – spend (time); **ayama(tsu)** – err; **ayama(chi)** – error

過度	kado	excessive, too much	377
通過	tsūka	passage, transit	150
過半数	kahansū	majority, more than half	88, 225
食べ過ぎる	tabesugiru	eat too much, overeat	322

414 去 〔土 3b 丿 1c 丶 1d〕

KYO, KO, sa(ru) – leave, move away; pass, elapse

去年	kyonen	last year	45
死去	shikyo	death	85
去来	kyorai	coming and going	69
過去	kako	past	413
立ち去る	tachisaru	leave, go away	121

415

辶 口 宀
2q 3d 2j

TEKI – fit, be suitable

適当	tekitō	suitable, appropriate	77
適度	tekido	to a proper degree, moderate	377
適切	tekisetsu	pertinent, appropriate	39
適用	tekiyō	application (of a rule)	107
適合	tekigō	conformity, compatibility	159

416

夂 口 宀
4i 3d 2j

TEKI, kataki – enemy, opponent, competitor

宿敵	shukuteki	old/hereditary enemy	179
強敵	kyōteki	powerful foe, formidable rival	217
敵意	tekii	enmity, hostility	132
敵対	tekitai	hostility, antagonism	365
不敵	futeki	fearless, daring	94

417

禾 王 口
5d 4f 3d

TEI, hodo – degree, extent

程度	teido	degree, extent, grade	377
過程	katei	a process	413
工程	kōtei	progress of the work; manufacturing process	139
日程	nittei	schedule for the day	5
音程	ontei	musical interval, step	347

418

糸 冂 一
6a 2r 1a3

SO, kumi – group, crew, class, gang; **ku(mu)** – put together

組成	sosei	composition, makeup	261
番組	bangumi	(TV) program	185
労働組合	rōdō kumiai	labor union	233, 232, 159
組み立て	kumitate	construction; assembling	121
組み合わせる	kumiawaseru	combine, fit together	159

419	女 口 一 3e 3s 1a	**YŌ** – main point, necessity; **i(ru)** – need, be necessary			
		重 要	*jūyō*	important	227
		主 要	*shuyō*	principal, major	155
		要 点	*yōten*	main point, gist	169
		要 素	*yōso*	element, factor	271
		要 約	*yōyaku*	summary	211

420	目 ハ 一 5c 2o 1a	**GU** – tool			
		具 体 的	*gutaiteki*	concrete, specific	61, 210
		道 具	*dōgu*	tool, implement	149
		家 具	*kagu*	furniture	165
		金 具	*kanagu*	metal fitting	23
		不 具	*fugu*	deformity, crippled	94

421	亻 口 一 2a 3s 1a	**KA, atai** – price, value			
		物 価	*bukka*	price (of commodities)	79
		米 価	*beika*	price of rice	224
		単 価	*tanka*	unit price	300
		定 価	*teika*	fixed/list price	355
		現 金 正 価	*genkin seika*	cash price	298, 23, 275

422	十 目 ハ 2k 5c 2o	**SHIN** – truth, genuineness, reality; **ma** – true, pure, exactly			
		真 実	*shinjitsu*	the truth, a fact	203
		真 理	*shinri*	truth	143
		真 相	*shinsō*	the truth, the facts	146
		真 空	*shinkū*	vacuum	140
		真 っ 暗	*makkura*	pitch-dark	348

423	十 目 丨 2k 5c 1b	**CHOKU, JIKI** – honest, frank, direct; **nao(su)** – fix, correct; **nao(ru)** – be fixed, corrected; **tada(chi ni)** – immediately

直線　　　　chokusen　　　straight line　　　　　　　　　　　299
直前/後　　choku-zen/go　immediately before/after　　　47, 48
正直　　　　shōjiki　　　　honest, upright　　　　　　　　　275
書き直す　　kakinaosu　　 write over again, rewrite　　　　131

直　直　直

直　直　直

424	木 目 十 4a 5c 2k	**SHOKU, u(eru)** – plant; **u(waru)** – be planted

植物　　　　shokubutsu　　a plant　　　　　　　　　　　　　79
動植物　　　dōshokubutsu　animals and plants　　　　　231, 79
植民地　　　shokuminchi　　colony　　　　　　　　　　177, 118
植木　　　　ueki　　　　　　garden/potted plant　　　　　　22
田植え　　　taue　　　　　　rice planting　　　　　　　　　35

植　植　植

植　植　植

425	亻 目 十 2a 5c 2k	**CHI, ne, atai** – value, price

価値　　　　kachi　　　　value　　　　　　　　　　　　　　421
値うち　　　neuchi　　　value; public estimation
値段　　　　nedan　　　price　　　　　　　　　　　　　　362
値上げ　　　neage　　　price increase　　　　　　　　　　32
値切る　　　negiru　　　haggle over the price, bargain　　39

値　値　値

値　値　値

426	罒 目 十 5g 5c 2k	**CHI, o(ku)** – put, set; leave behind/as is

位置　　　　ichi　　　　　　position, location　　　　　　　122
置き物　　　okimono　　　　ornament; figurehead　　　　　79
物置き　　　monooki　　　　storeroom, shed　　　　　　　79
前置き　　　maeoki　　　　 introductory remarks, preface　47
一日置き　　ichinichioki　　 every other day　　　　　　　　2, 5

置　置　置

置　置　置

427

⺉巾一
2f 3f 1a2

SEI – system; regulations

制度	seido	system	377
税制	zeisei	system of taxation	399
新制	shinsei	new order, reorganization	174
強制	kyōsei	compulsion, force	217
管制	kansei	control	328

428

衤巾⺉
5e 3f 2f

SEI – produce, manufacture, make

製作	seisaku	a work, production	360
製品	seihin	product	230
製鉄	seitetsu	iron manufacturing	312
木製	mokusei	wooden, made of wood	22
日本製	nihonsei	Japanese-made, Made in Japan	5, 25

429

土卜亻
3b 2m 2a

SŌ, hashi(ru) – run

走路	sōro	(race) track, course	151
走行時間	sōkō jikan	travel time	68, 42, 43
走り回る	hashirimawaru	run around	90
走り書き	hashirigaki	flowing/hasty handwriting	131
口走る	kuchibashiru	babble, blurt out	54

430

彳土卜
3i 3b 2m

TO – on foot; companions; vain, useless

生徒	seito	pupil, student	44
教徒	kyōto	believer, adherent	245
使徒	shito	apostle	331
徒手	toshu	empty-handed; penniless	57
徒労	torō	vain effort	233

431	ⸯ ト 一 3n 2m 1a	**HO, BU, [FU], aru(ku), ayu(mu)** – walk		
歩		歩道	hodō	footpath, sidewalk	149
		歩行者	hokōsha	pedestrian	68, 164
		一歩	ippo	a step	2
		歩調	hochō	pace, step	342
		歩合	buai	rate, percentage; commission	159

432	氵 ⸯ ト 3a 3n 2m	**SHŌ** – cross over; have to do with		
渉		交渉	kōshō	negotiations	114

433	車 一 ノ 7c 1a2 1c	**TEN, koro(bu/garu/geru)** – roll over, fall down; **koro(gasu)** – roll, knock down		
転		自転車	jitensha	bicycle	62, 133
		回転	kaiten	rotation, revolution	90
		空転	kūten	idling (of an engine)	140
		転任	tennin	transfer of assignments/personnel	334

434	イ 一 ノ 2a 1a2 1c	**DEN, tsuta(eru)** – transmit, impart; **tsuta(waru)** – be transmitted, imparted; **tsuta(u)** – go along		
伝		伝記	denki	biography	371
		伝説	densetsu	legend, folklore	400
		伝動	dendō	evangelism, missionary work	149
		手伝い	tetsudai	help, helper	57

435 艹 一 丿 3k 1a2 1c	**GEI** – art, craft		
芸者	geisha	geisha	164
芸術	geijutsu	art	187
文芸	bungei	literary art, literature	111
演芸	engei	performance, entertainment	344
民芸	mingei	folkcraft	177

芸

436 隹 木 8c 4a	**SHŪ**, atsu(maru/meru) – (intr./tr.) gather; tsudo(u) – (intr.) gather		
集金	shūkin	bill collecting	23
集中	shūchū	concentration	28
全集	zenshū	the complete works	89
特集	tokushū	special edition	282
万葉集	Man'yōshū	(Japan's oldest anthology of poems)	16, 253

集

437 辶 隹 2q 8c	**SHIN**, susu(mu) – advance, progress; susu(meru) – advance, promote		
進歩	shinpo	progress, improvement	431
進行	shinkō	progress, onward movement	68
前進	zenshin	advance, forward movement	47
先進国	senshinkoku	developed/advanced country	50, 40

進

438 宀 車 2i 7c	**GUN** – army, troops, war		
軍人	gunjin	soldier, military man	1
軍事	gunji	military affairs, military	80
海軍	kaigun	navy	117
敵軍	tekigun	enemy army/troops	416
軍国主義	gunkoku shugi	militarism	40, 155, 291

軍

219

439	辶 車 宀	*UN* – fate, luck; *hako(bu)* – carry, transport	
	2q 7c 2i	運転手　　*untenshu*　　driver, chauffeur	433, 57
		(労働) 運動　*(rōdō) undō*　(labor) movement	233, 232, 231
		運動不足　*undōbusoku*　lack of exercise	231, 94, 58
		運河　　　*unga*　　canal	389
		不運　　　*fuun*　　misfortune	94

運

440	辶 車	*REN* – group, accompaniment; *tsu(reru)* – take (someone); *tsura(naru)* – stand in a row;	
	2q 7c	*tsura(neru)* – link, put in a row	
		連続　　　*renzoku*　　series, continuity	243
		連合　　　*rengō*　　combination, league, coalition	159
		国連　　　*kokuren*　　United Nations	40
		家族連れ　*kazokuzure*　with the family	165, 221

連

441	辶 ⸀ 亻	*SŌ, oku(ru)* – send	
	2q 2o 2a	運送　　　*unsō*　　transport, shipment	439
		回送　　　*kaisō*　　forwarding	90
		送金　　　*sōkin*　　remittance	23
		送別会　　*sōbetsukai*　going-away/farewell party	267, 158
		見送る　　*miokuru*　　see (someone) off; escort	63

送

442	辶 厂 又	*HEN, kae(ru/su)* – (intr./tr.) return	
	2q 2p 2h	返事　　　*henji*　　reply	80
		返信用葉書　*henshin'yō hagaki*　reply postcard	157, 107, 253, 131
		見返す　　*mikaesu*　　look back; triumph over (an old enemy)	63
		読み返す　*yomikaesu*　reread	244
		送り返す　*okurikaesu*　send back	441

返

443	土 厂 又
	3b 2p 2h

HAN, saka – slope, hill

急 な 坂	kyū na saka	steep slope/hill	303
坂 道	sakamichi	road on a slope	149
上 り 坂	noborizaka	ascent	32
下 り 坂	kudarizaka	descent; decline	31
赤 坂	Akasaka	(area of Tokyo)	207

坂

444	辶 ⺌ 屮
	2q 2o 3o

GYAKU – reverse, inverse, opposite; treason; *saka* – reverse, inverse; *saka(rau)* – be contrary (to)

逆 転	gyakuten	reversal	433
逆 説	gyakusetsu	paradox	400
反 逆	hangyaku	treason	324
逆 立 つ	sakadatsu	stand on end	121

逆

445	辶 厂 一
	2q 2p 1a

KIN, chika(i) – near, close

近 所	kinjo	vicinity, neighborhood	153
付 近	fukin	vicinity, environs	192
最 近	saikin	recent; most recent, latest	263
近 代	kindai	modern times, modern	256
近 道	chikamichi	shortcut, shorter way	149

近

446	辶 土 口
	2q 3b 3d

EN, [ON], tō(i) – far, distant

遠 方	enpō	great distance, (in) the distance	70
遠 近 法	enkinhō	(law of) perspective	445, 123
遠 足	ensoku	excursion, outing	58
遠 心 力	enshinryoku	centrifugal force	97, 100
遠 回 し	tōmawashi	indirect, roundabout	90

遠

447	口 土 口 3s 3b 3d	**EN, sono** – garden		

園

公園	kōen	(public) park	126
動物園	dōbutsuen	zoo	231, 79
植物園	shokubutsuen	botanical garden	424, 79
学園	gakuen	educational institution, academy	109
楽園	rakuen	paradise	358

448	辶 王 土 2q 4f 3b	**TATSU** – reach, arrive at		

達

上達	jōtatsu	progress; proficiency	32
発達	hattatsu	development	96
達成	tassei	achieve, attain	261
達人	tatsujin	expert, master	1
友達	tomodachi	friend	264

449	月 艹 ソ 4b 3k 2o	**KI, [GO]** – time, period, term		

期

期間	kikan	period of time, term	43
定期	teiki	fixed period	355
過渡期	katoki	transition period	413, 378
学期	gakki	semester, trimester, school term	109
短期大学	tanki daigaku	junior college	215, 26, 109

450	土 艹 ソ 3b 3k 2o	**KI, moto, motoi** – basis, foundation, origin		

基

基本	kihon	basis, fundamentals; standard	25
基金	kikin	fund, endowment	23
基地	kichi	(military) base	118
基石	kiseki	foundation stone, cornerstone	78
基調	kichō	keynote	342

451	扌 土 十	**JI, mo(tsu)** – have, possess; hold, maintain
	3c 3b 2k	

支持	shiji	support	318
持続	jizoku	continuance, maintenance	243
持ち主	mochinushi	owner, possessor	155
金持ち	kanemochi	rich person	23
気持ち	kimochi	mood, feeling	134

452	彳 土 十	**TAI, ma(tsu)** – wait for
	3i 3b 2k	

期待	kitai	expectation, anticipation	449
特待	tokutai	special treatment, distinction	282
待ち合い室	machiaishitsu	waiting room	159, 166
待ち合わせる	machiawaseru	wait for (as previously arranged)	159
待ちほうけ	machibōke	getting stood up	

453	彳	**KAI** – shellfish (cf. No. 240); be in between, mediate
	2a 1b2	

介入	kainyū	intervention	52
介在	kaizai	lie/stand/come between	268
魚介	gyokai	fish and shellfish, marine products	290
一介の	ikkai no	mere, only	2

454	田 彳	**KAI** – world
	5f 2a 1b2	

世界	sekai	world	252
世界史	sekaishi	world history	252, 332
学界	gakkai	academic world	109
外界	gaikai	external world, outside	83
下界	gekai	this world, the earth below	31

455	扌 口 刂
	3c 3d 2f

SHŌ, mane(ku) – beckon to, invite, cause

| 招待 | shōtai | invitation | 452 |
| 手招き | temaneki | beckoning | 57 |

招　招　招

招　招　招

456	糸 口 刂
	6a 3d 2f

SHŌ – introduction

| 紹介 | shōkai | introduction, presentation | 453 |
| 自己紹介 | jiko shōkai | introduce oneself | 62, 370, 453 |

紹　紹　紹

紹　紹　紹

457	宀 艹 冫
	3m 3k 2o

KAN – coldest season, coldness; **samu(i)** – cold

寒気	kanki	the cold	134
寒中	kanchū	the cold season	28
極寒	gokkan	severe cold	336
寒村	kanson	poor/lonely village	191
寒空	samuzora	wintry sky, cold weather	140

寒　寒　寒

寒　寒　寒

458	糸 夂 丶
	6a 4i 1d2

SHŪ, o(waru/eru) – come/bring to an end

最終	saishū	last	263
終戦	shūsen	end of the war	301
終点	shūten	end of the line, last stop, terminus	169
終身	shūshin	for life, lifelong	59
終日	shūjitsu	all day long	5

終　終　終

終　終　終

459	夂丶 4i 1d2	***TŌ, fuyu*** – winter			
		立冬	*rittō*	first day of winter	121
		真冬	*mafuyu*	midwinter, the dead of winter	422
		冬向き	*fumuki*	for winter	199
		冬物	*fuyumono*	winter clothing	79
		冬空	*fuyuzora*	winter sky	140

460	日 亻 一 4c 2a 1a3	***SHUN, haru*** – spring			
		春分 (の日)	*shunbun (no hi)*	vernal equinox	38, 5
		立春	*risshun*	beginning of spring	121
		青春	*seishun*	springtime of life, youth	208
		売春	*baishun*	prostitution	239
		春画	*shunga*	obscene picture, pornography	343

461	夂目一 4i 5c 1a	***KA, [GE], natsu*** – summer			
		夏期	*kaki*	the summer period	449
		立夏	*rikka*	beginning of summer	121
		真夏	*manatsu*	midsummer, height of summer	422
		夏物	*natsumono*	summer clothing	79
		夏休み	*natsuyasumi*	summer vacation	60

462	禾火 5d 4d	***SHŪ, aki*** – fall, autumn			
		春夏秋冬	*shunkashūtō*	all the year round	460, 461, 459
		春秋	*shunjū*	spring and autumn; years, age	460
		秋分 (の日)	*shūbun (no hi)*	autumnal equinox	38, 5
		秋気	*shūki*	the autumn air	134
		秋風	*akikaze*	autumn breeze	29

463	口 日 丶 2e 4c 1d	**SOKU** – immediately; conform (to); namely, i.e.		
		即時 *sokuji* instantly, immediately, on the spot		42
		即日 *sokujitsu* on the same day		5
		即金 *sokkin* cash; payment in cash		23
		即席 *sokuseki* extemporaneous, impromptu		379
		即興 *sokkyō* improvised, ad-lib		368

464	⺮ 日 口 6f 4c 2e	**SETSU, [SECHI]** – season; occasion; section, paragraph; verse; *fushi* – joint, knuckle; melody; point		
		時節 *jisetsu* time of year; the times		42
		調節 *chōsetsu* adjustment, regulation		342
		使節 *shisetsu* envoy, mission		331
		節約 *setsuyaku* economizing, thrift		211

465	禾 子 5d 2c	**KI** – season		
		季節 *kisetsu* season, time of year		464
		四季 *shiki* the 4 seasons		6
		季節風 *kisetsufū* seasonal wind, monsoon		464, 29
		季節外れ *kisetsuhazure* out of season		464, 83
		季語 *kigo* word indicating the season (in haiku)		67

466	禾 女 5d 3e	**I** – entrust		
		委任 *inin* trust, mandate, authorization		334
		委員 *iin* committee member		163
		委員会 *iinkai* committee		163, 158

467	氵 月 口
	3a 4b 3d

KO, mizuumi – lake

湖 水	*kosui*	lake	21
火 口 湖	*kakōko*	crater lake	20, 54
湖 面	*komen*	surface of a lake	274
山 中 湖	*Yamanaka-ko*	(lake near Mt. Fuji)	34, 28
十 和 田 湖	*Towada-ko*	(lake in Tohoku)	12, 124, 35

468	氵 月 日
	3a 4b 4c

CHŌ, shio – tide; salt water; opportunity

満 潮	*manchō*	high tide	201
潮 流	*chōryū*	tidal current; trend of the times	247
風 潮	*fūchō*	tide; tendency, trend	29
潮 時	*shiodoki*	favorable tide; opportunity	42
黒 潮	*Kuroshio*	Japan Current	206

469	月 日 十
	4b 4c 2k2

CHŌ – morning; dynasty; *asa* – morning

朝 食	*chōshoku*	breakfast	322
平 安 朝	*Heianchō*	Heian period (794-1185)	202, 105
朝 日	*asahi*	morning/rising sun	5
毎 朝	*maiasa*	every morning	116
今 朝	*kesa, konchō*	this morning	51

470	日 尸 一
	4c 3r 1a

CHŪ, hiru – daytime, noon

昼 食	*chūshoku*	lunch	322
白 昼 に	*hakuchū ni*	in broad daylight	205
昼 飯	*hirumeshi*	lunch	325
昼 間	*hiruma*	daytime	43
昼 休 み	*hiruyasumi*	lunch break, noon recess	60

471	亠 亻 夕 2j 2a 2n	**YA, yoru, yo** – night			
		昼夜	chūya	day and night	470
		今夜	kon'ya	tonight	51
		夜行	yakō	traveling by night; night train	68
		夜学	yagaku	evening class	109
		夜明け	yoake	dawn, daybreak	18

472	氵 亠 亻 3a 2j 2a	**EKI** – liquid, fluid			
		液体	ekitai	liquid, fluid	61
		液化	ekika	liquefaction	254
		だ液	daeki	saliva	

473	勹 土 冂 2n 3b 2r	**KAKU** – angle, corner; **kado** – corner, angle; **tsuno** – horn, antlers			
		角度	kakudo	degrees of an angle, angle	377
		三角(形)	sankaku(kei)	triangle	4,395
		直角	chokkaku	right angle	423
		街角	machikado	street corner	186

474	牛 土 勹 4g 3b 2n	**KAI, GE, to(ku)** – untie; solve; **to(keru)** – come loose; be solved; **to(kasu)** – comb			
		理解	rikai	understanding	143
		解説	kaisetsu	explanation, commentary	400
		解決	kaiketsu	solution, settlement	356
		和解	wakai	compromise	124
		解任	kainin	dismissal, release	304

228

475

草 米 一
3k 6b 1a

KIKU – chrysanthemum

白 菊	*shiragiku*	white chrysanthemum	205
菊 の 花	*kiku no hana*	chrysanthemum	255
菊 作 り	*kikuzukuri*	chrysanthemum growing	360
菊 人 形	*kikuningyō*	chrysanthemum doll	1,395
菊 地	*Kikuchi*	(surname)	118

476

米 冂 亻
6b 2r 2a

Ō, oku – interior

奥 義	*ōgi, okugi*	secrets, hidden mysteries	291
奥 行 き	*okuyuki*	depth (vs. height and width)	68
山 奥	*yamaoku*	deep in the mountains	34
奥 付 け	*okuzuke*	colophon	192
奥 さ ん	*okusan*	wife; ma'am	

477

卜 一 丨
2m 1a 1b

SHI, to(maru/meru) – come/bring to a stop

終 止	*shūshi*	termination, end	458
休 止	*kyūshi*	pause, suspension	60
通 行 止 め	*tsūkōdome*	Road Closed, No Thoroughfare	150, 68
口 止 め 料	*kuchidomeryō*	hush money	54, 319
足 止 め	*ashidome*	keep indoors, confinement	58

478

米 卜 一
6b 2m 1a

SHI, ha – tooth

門/犬 歯	*mon/kenshi*	incisor/canine	161, 280
義 歯	*gishi*	false teeth, dentures	291
歯 科 医	*shikai*	dentist	319, 220
歯 医 者	*haisha*	dentist	220, 164
歯 車	*haguruma*	toothed wheel, gear	133

479	戈 ⺍ ト 4n 3n 2m	**SAI** – year, years old; **[SEI]** – year	
		満四歳	*man'yonsai*	4 (full) years old	201, 6
		二十歳	*hatachi*	20 years old	3, 12
		万歳	*banzai*	Hurrah! Long live...!	16
		歳月	*saigetsu*	time, years	17
		歳入歳出	*sainyū-saishutsu*	yearly revenue and expenditure	52, 53

480	厂 木 止 2p 4a2 2m	**REKI** – continuation, passing of time	
		歴史	*rekishi*	history	332
		学歴	*gakureki*	school career, academic background	109
		前歴	*zenreki*	one's personal history, background	47
		歴任	*rekinin*	successive holding of various posts	334

481	イ 止 一 2a 2m 1a	**KI, kuwada(teru)** – plan, undertake, attempt	
		企業	*kigyō*	enterprise, undertaking	279
		中小企業	*chūshō kigyō*	small- and medium-size enterprises	28, 27, 279
		企画	*kikaku*	planning, plan	343
		企図	*kito*	plan, project, scheme	339

482	ネ 木 4e 4a2	**KIN** – prohibition	
		禁止	*kinshi*	prohibition	. 477
		解禁	*kaikin*	lifting of a ban	474
		禁制	*kinsei*	prohibition, ban	427
		禁物	*kinmotsu*	forbidden things, taboo	79
		発禁	*hakkin*	prohibition of sale	96

483	攵 卜 一 4i 2m 1a	**SEI, [SHŌ], matsurigoto** – government, rule		
		政局	*seikyoku*	political situation	170
		行政	*gyōsei*	administration	68
		内政	*naisei*	domestic politics, internal affairs	84
		市政	*shisei*	municipal government	181
		家政	*kasei*	management of a household, housekeeping	165

政 　政　政

政 政 政

484	言 卜 一 7a 2m 1a2	**SHŌ** – proof, evidence, certificate		
		証明	*shōmei*	proof, testimony, corroboration	18
		証人	*shōnin*	witness	1
		証言	*shōgen*	testimony	66
		反証	*hanshō*	counterproof, counterevidence	324
		内証	*naisho, naishō*	secret	84

証 　証　証

証 証 証

485	糸 吉 口 6a 3p 3d	**KETSU, musu(bu)** – tie, bind; conclude (a contract); bear (fruit); **yu(waeru)** – tie; **yu(u)** – do up (one's hair)		
		結論	*ketsuron*	conclusion	293
		結成	*kessei*	formation, organization	261
		結合	*ketsugō*	union, combination	159
		終結	*shūketsu*	conclusion, termination	458

結 　結　結

結 結 結

486	扌 立 女 3c 5b 3e	**SETSU** – touch, contact; **tsu(gu)** – join together		
		直接	*chokusetsu*	direct	423
		間接	*kansetsu*	indirect	43
		面接	*mensetsu*	interview	274
		接続	*setsuzoku*	connection, joining	243
		接待	*settai*	reception, welcome; serving, offering	452

接 　接　接

接 接 接

487 一日木 (1a) 4c 4a	**KA** – fruit; result; **ha(tasu)** – carry out, complete; **ha(teru)** – come to an end; **ha(te)** – end, limit; result

結果	kekka	result	485
成果	seika	result	261
果実	kajitsu	fruit	203
果物	kudamono	fruit	79

果

488 言日木 7a 4c 4a	**KA** – lesson; section

第一課	daiikka	Lesson 1	404, 2
課目	kamoku	subject (in school)	55
課程	katei	course, curriculum	417
課長	kachō	section chief	95
人事課	jinjika	personnel section	1, 80

課

489 亻木口 2a 4a 3d	**HO, tamo(tsu)** – keep, preserve, maintain

保証	hoshō	guarantee, warranty	484
保証人	hoshōnin	guarantor, sponsor	484, 1
保存	hozon	preservation	269
保育所	hoikusho, hoikujo	daycare nursery	246, 153
保養所	hoyōsho, hoyōjo	sanatorium, rest home	402, 153

保

490 宀十、 3m 2k 1d	**SHU, [SU], mamo(ru)** – protect; obey, abide by; **mori** – babysitter, (lighthouse) keeper

保守的	hoshuteki	conservative	489, 210
子守	komori	baby-sitting; baby-sitter, nursemaid	103
子守歌	komoriuta	lullaby	103, 392
見守る	mimamoru	keep watch over; stare at	63
お守り	omamori	charm, amulet	

守

491 団 口 十 丶
3s 2k 1d

DAN, [TON] – group

団体 (旅行)	dantai (ryokō)	group (tour)	61, 222, 68
集団	shūdan	group, mass	436
団地	danchi	public housing development/complex	118
団結	danketsu	unity, solidarity	485
師団	shidan	(army) division	409

492 台 口 ノ 丶
3d 1c 1d

DAI, TAI – stand, pedestal, platform, plateau

台所	daidokoro	kitchen	153
天文台	tenmondai	observatory	141, 111
高台	takadai	high ground, a height	190
台本	daihon	script, screenplay, libretto	25
台風	taifū	typhoon	29

493 治 氵 口 ノ
3a 3d 1c

JI, CHI – peace; government; healing; *osa(meru)* – govern; suppress; *osa(maru)* – be at peace, quelled; *nao(ru/su)* – (intr./tr.) heal

政治	seiji	politics	483
自治	jichi	self-government, autonomy	62
明治時代	Meiji jidai	Meiji era (1868–1912)	18, 42, 256

494 始 女 口 ノ
3e 3d 1c

SHI, haji(maru/meru) – (intr./tr.) start, begin

始末	shimatsu	circumstances; management, disposal	305
始終	shijū	from first to last, all the while	458
始発	shihatsu	the first (train) departure	96
開始	kaishi	beginning, opening	396
原始的	genshiteki	primitive, original	136, 210

495	⺌ 口 冖 3n 3d 2i	**TŌ** – party, faction			
		政党	seitō	political party	483
		野党	yatō	party out of power, the opposition	236
		党員/首	tōin/shu	party member/leader	163, 148
		徒党	totō	confederates, clique, conspiracy	430
		社会党	Shakaitō	Socialist Party	308, 158

党

496	⺌ 口 土 3n 3d 3b	**DŌ** – temple; hall			
		食堂	shokudō	dining hall, restaurant	322
		能楽堂	nōgakudō	Noh theater	386, 358
		公会堂	kōkaidō	public hall, community center	126, 158
		本堂	hondō	main temple	25
		国会議事堂	kokkai gijidō	Diet Building	40, 158, 292, 80

堂

497	⺌ 口 巾 3n 3d 3f	**JŌ, tsune** – normal, usual, continual; **toko-** – ever-, always			
		日常生活	nichijō seikatsu	everyday life	5, 44, 237
		正常	seijō	normal	275
		通常	tsūjō	ordinary, usual	150
		常任委員	jōnin iin	member of a standing committee	334, 466, 163

常

498	一 卜 丨 (1a5) 2m 1b	**HI** – mistake; (prefix) non-, un-			
		非常口	hijōguchi	emergency exit	497, 54
		非常事態	hijō jitai	state of emergency	497, 80, 387
		非公開	hikōkai	not open to the public, private	126, 396
		非人間的	hiningenteki	inhuman, impersonal	1, 43, 210
		非合法	higōhō	illegal	159, 123

非

499	⺌ 口 扌	**SHŌ** – palm of the hand; administer		
	3n 3d 3c	合掌	*gasshō*	clasp one's hands (in prayer)	159
		掌中	*shōchū*	pocket (edition), in the hand	28
		掌中の玉	*shōchū no tama*	apple of one's eye, one's jewel	28, 295
		車掌	*shashō*	(train) conductor	133

掌

500	⺌ 貝 口	**SHŌ** – prize; praise		
	3n 7b 3d	文学賞	*bungaku-shō*	prize for literature	111, 109
		ノーベル賞	*Nōberu-shō*	Nobel Prize	
		賞品	*shōhin*	a prize	230
		賞金	*shōkin*	cash prize, prize money	23
		受賞者	*jushōsha*	prizewinner	260, 164

賞

501	一 朩 口	**SOKU, taba** – bundle, sheaf		
	(1a) 4a 3s	一束	*issoku, hitotaba*	a bundle	2
		約束	*yakusoku*	promise, appointment	211
		結束	*kessoku*	unity, union, bond	485
		花束	*hanataba*	bouquet	255
		束ねる	*tabaneru*	tie in a bundle; control	

束

502	辶 朩 口	**SOKU, haya(i), sumi(yaka)** – fast, quick, prompt; **haya(meru)** – quicken, accelerate		
	2q 4a 3s	速力/度	*soku-ryoku/do*	speed, velocity	100, 377
		高速道路	*kōsoku dōro*	expressway, freeway	190, 149, 151
		速達	*sokutatsu*	special/express delivery	448
		速記	*sokki*	shorthand, stenography	371

速

503	攵木 口 4i 4a 3s	**SEI**, *totono(eru)* – put in order, prepare; *totono(u)* – be put in order, prepared

整理　　　seiri　　　　arrangement, adjustment　　　　　　　　143
調整　　　chōsei　　　adjustment, modulation　　　　　　　　342
整形外科　seikei geka　plastic surgery　　　　　　　395, 83, 320
整数　　　seisū　　　　integer　　　　　　　　　　　　　　　225

整　整　整

整　整　整

504	广亻 十 3q 2a 2k	**FU** – storehouse; government office; capital city

政府　　　seifu　　　　government　　　　　　　　　　　　483
無政府　　museifu　　　anarchy　　　　　　　　　　　　93, 483
首府　　　shufu　　　　the capital　　　　　　　　　　　　148
京都府　　Kyōto-fu　　Kyoto Prefecture　　　　　　　189, 188
都道府県　todōfuken　　the Japanese prefectures　　188, 149, 194

府　府　府

府　府　府

505	⺮亻 十 6f 2a 2k	**FU** – sign, mark; amulet

切符　　　　　kippu　　　　ticket　　　　　　　　　　　　　　　39
切符売り場　　kippu uriba　ticket office/window　　　　39, 239, 154
音符　　　　　onpu　　　　diacritical mark; musical note　　　　347
符号　　　　　fugō　　　　mark, symbol　　　　　　　　　　　266
符合　　　　　fugō　　　　coincidence, agreement, correspondence　159

符　符　符

符　符　符

506	一 刂亻 1a2 2f 2a	**KEN** – ticket, certificate

入場券　　　nyūjōken　　admission ticket　　　　　　　52, 154
旅券　　　　ryoken　　　passport　　　　　　　　　　　　222
回数券　　　kaisūken　　coupon ticket　　　　　　　　90, 225
定期券　　　teikiken　　commutation ticket, (train) pass　355, 449
(有価)証券　(yūka) shōken　securities　　　　　265, 421, 484

券　券　券

券　券　券

507	一 イ 丨 1a4 2a 1b	**KAN, maki** – roll, reel; volume; **ma(ku)** – roll, wind	
		上/中/下 巻　*jō/chū/ge-kan*　first/middle/last volume	32, 28, 31
		第一巻　*daiikkan*　Volume 1	404, 2
		絵巻(物)　*emaki(mono)*　picture scroll	345, 79
		葉巻　*hamaki*　cigar	253
		取り巻く　*torimaku*　surround, encircle	65

巻

508	囗 イ 一 3s 2a 1a4	**KEN** – circle, range, sphere	
		共産圏　*kyōsanken*　the Communist bloc/countries	196, 278
		極地圏　*kyokuchiken*　polar region	336, 118
		北/南極圏　*hok/nan-kyokuken*　Arctic/Antarctic Circle	73, 74, 336
		首都圏　*shutoken*　the capital region	148, 188
		圏内/外　*kennai/gai*　within/outside the range (of)	84, 83

圏

509	月 力 イ 4b 2g 2a	**SHŌ, ka(tsu)** – win; **masa(ru)** – be superior (to)	
		勝利　*shōri*　victory	329
		勝(利)者　*shō(ri)sha*　victor, winner	329, 164
		決勝　*kesshō*　decision (of a competition)	356
		連勝　*renshō*　series of victories, winning streak	440
		勝ち通す　*kachitōsu*　win successive victories	150

勝

510	⺈ 貝 2n 7b	**FU, ma(keru)** – be defeated, lose; give a discount; **ma(kasu)** – beat, defeat; **o(u)** – carry, bear; owe	
		勝負　*shōbu*　victory or defeat; game, match	509
		自負　*jifu*　conceit, self-importance	62
		負けん気　*makenki*　unyielding/competitive spirit	134
		負け犬　*makeinu*　loser	280

負

511	貝 攵 7b 4i	***HAI, yabu(reru)*** – be defeated, beaten, frustrated		
		敗北	*haiboku*	defeat	73
		勝敗	*shōhai*	victory or defeat, outcome	509
		失敗	*shippai*	failure, blunder	311
		敗戦	*haisen*	lost battle, defeat	301
		敗者	*haisha*	the defeated, loser	164

512	方 攵 4h 4i	***HŌ, hana(tsu)*** – set free, release; fire (a gun); emit; ***hana(su)*** – set free, release; ***hana(reru)*** – get free of		
		解放	*kaihō*	liberation, emancipation	474
		放送	*hōsō*	(radio/TV) broadcasting	441
		放火	*hōka*	arson	20
		放置	*hōchi*	let alone, leave as is, leave to chance	426

513	阝 方 2d 4h	***BŌ, fuse(gu)*** – defend/protect from, prevent		
		防止	*bōshi*	prevention, keeping in check	477
		予防	*yobō*	prevention, precaution	393
		国防	*kokubō*	national defense	40
		防火	*bōka*	fire prevention/fighting	20
		防水	*bōsui*	waterproof, watertight	21

514	攵 一 丨 4i 1a2 1b	***KAI, arata(meru)*** – alter, renew, reform; ***arata(maru)*** – be altered, renewed, corrected		
		改正	*kaisei*	improvement; revision	275
		改良	*kairyō*	improvement, reform	321
		改新	*kaishin*	renovation, reformation	174
		改名	*kaimei*	changing one's name	82

515

酉 7e　一 1a2　丨 1b

配

HAI, kuba(ru) – distribute, pass out

心配	*shinpai*	worry, concern	97
支配	*shihai*	management, administration, rule	318
配達	*haitatsu*	deliver	448
配置	*haichi*	arrangement, placement	426
気配	*kehai*	sign, indication	134

516

酉 7e　夂 4i　丷 2o

酸

SAN, su(i) – acid, sour

酸味	*sanmi*	acidity, sourness	307
酸性	*sansei*	acidity	98
酸化	*sanka*	oxidation	254
酸素	*sanso*	oxygen	271
青酸	*seisan*	prussic acid, hydrogen cyanide	208

517

氵 3a　酉 7e

酒

SHU, sake, [saka] – saké, rice wine, liquor

日本酒	*nihonshu*	saké Japanese rice wine	5, 25
ぶどう酒	*budōshu*	(grape) wine	
禁酒	*kinshu*	abstinence from drink; temperance	482
酒屋	*sakaya*	wine dealer, liquor store	167
酒場	*sakaba*	bar, saloon, tavern	154

518

宀 3m　土 3b　口 3d

害

GAI – injury, harm, damage

公害	*kōgai*	pollution	126
水害	*suigai*	flood damage, flooding	21
損害	*songai*	injury, loss	350
利害	*rigai*	advantages and disadvantages, interests	329
妨害	*bōgai*	hindrance, obstruction	513

519	刂 宀 土 2f 3m 3b	**KATSU, wa(ru)** – divide, separate, split; **wa(reru)** – break, crack/split apart; **wari** – proportion; profit; 10 percent; **sa(ku)** – cut up; separate; spare (time)

分 割	bunkatsu	division, partitioning	38
割 合	wariai	rate, proportion, percentage	159
割 引 き	waribiki	discount	216

520	ノ 心 1c 4k	**HITSU, kanara(zu)** – surely, (be) sure (to), without fail

必 要	hitsuyō	necessary, requisite	419
必 死	hisshi	certain death; desperation	85
必 読	hitsudoku	required reading	244
必 勝	hisshō	sure victory	509
必 ず し も …な い	kanarazushimo … nai	not necessarily	

521	宀 罒 心 3m 5g 4k	**KEN** – law

憲 法	kenpō	constitution	123
改 憲	kaiken	constitutional revision	514
憲 政	kensei	constitutional government	483
立 憲	rikken	constitutional	121
官 憲	kanken	the (government) authorities	326

522	一 土 丨 1a3 3b 1b2	**DOKU** – poison

毒 薬	dokuyaku	poison	359
有 毒	yūdoku	poisonous	265
中 毒	chūdoku	poisoning	28
毒 草	dokusō	poisonous plant	249
気 の 毒	kinodoku	pitiable, regrettable, unfortunate	134

523	一 木 艹
	1a 4a 3k

JŌ, no(ru) – get in/on, ride, take (a train); be fooled; **no(seru)** – let ride, take aboard; deceive, trick, take in

乗用車	jōyōsha	passenger car	107, 133
乗車券	jōshaken	(passenger) ticket	133, 506
乗組員	norikumiin	(ship's) crew	418, 163
乗っ取る	nottoru	take over, commandeer, hijack	65

乗 乗 乗

乗 乗 乗

524	阝 艹 十
	2d 3k 2k

YŪ – mail

郵便局	yūbinkyoku	post office	330, 170
郵便配達(人)	yūbin haitatsu(nin)	mailman	330, 515, 448, 1
郵便料金	yūbin ryōkin	postage	330, 319, 23
郵税	yūzei	postage	399
郵送料	yūsōryō	postage	441, 319

郵 郵 郵

郵 郵 郵

525	戈 一 丨
	4n 1a 1b

SHIKI – ceremony, rite; style, form, method; formula

正式	seishiki	prescribed form, formal	275
公式	kōshiki	formula (in mathematics); formal, official	126
様式	yōshiki	mode, style	403
方式	hōshiki	formula, mode; method, system	70
新式	shinshiki	new type	174

式 式 式

式 式 式

526	言 戈 一
	7a 4n 1a

SHI, kokoro(miru), tame(su) – give it a try, try out, attempt

試合	shiai	game, match	159
試作	shisaku	trial manufacture/cultivation	360
試食	shishoku	sample, taste	322
試運転	shiunten	trial run	439, 433
試金石	shikinseki	touchstone; test	23, 78

試 試 試

試 試 試

527	口 イ 一 3d4 2a 1a	**KI, utsuwa** – container, apparatus; capacity, ability		
		楽器	gakki	musical instrument	358
		器楽	kigaku	instrumental music	358
		器具	kigu	utensil, appliance, tool, apparatus	420
		食器	shokki	eating utensils	322
		不/無器用	(bu)kiyō	(not) dexterous	94, 93, 107

器　器　器　器

528	木 戈 イ 4a 4n 2a	**KI** – opportunity; machine; **hata** – loom		
		機関	kikan	engine; machinery, organ, medium	398
		制動機	seidōki	a brake	427, 231
		起重機	kijūki	crane	373, 227
		機能	kinō	a function	386
		機会	kikai	opportunity, occasion, chance	158

機　機　機　機

529	木 戈 艹 4a 4n 3k	**KAI** – fetters; machine		
		器械	kikai	instrument, apparatus, appliance	527
		機械	kikai	machine, machinery	528
		機械化	kikaika	mechanization	528, 254
		機械文明	kikai bunmei	technological civilization	528, 111, 18

械　械　械　械

530	一 丨 ノ 1a2 1b 1c3	**HI, to(bu)** – fly; **to(basu)** – let fly; skip over, omit		
		飛行	hikō	flight, aviation	68
		飛行機	hikōki	airplane	68, 528
		飛行場	hikōjō	airport	68, 154
		飛び石	tobiishi	stepping-stones	78
		飛び火	tobihi	flying sparks, leaping flames	20

飛　飛　飛　飛

531

木 口 亻
4a 3s 2a2

検

KEN – investigation, inspection

検事	kenji	public procurator/prosecutor	80
検定	kentei	official approval, inspection	355
検証	kenshō	verification, inspection	484
検死	kenshi	coroner's inquest, autopsy	85
点検	tenken	inspection, examination	169

検 検 検

検 検 検

532

馬 口 亻
10a 3s 2a2

験

KEN – effect; testing; [GEN] – beneficial effect

実験	jikken	experiment	203
試験	shiken	examination, test	526
入学試験	nyūgaku shiken	entrance exam	52, 109, 526
体験	taiken	experience	61
受験	juken	take a test/exam	260

験 験 験

験 験 験

533

阝 口 亻
2d 3s 2a2

険

KEN, kewa(shii) – steep, inaccessible; stern, harsh

保険	hoken	insurance	489
険悪	ken'aku	dangerous, threatening	304
険路	kenro	steep path	151
険しい路	kewashii michi	steep/treacherous road	149
険しい顔つき	kewashii kaotsuki	stern/fierce look	277

険 険 険

険 険 険

534

⺈ 厂 一
2n 2p 1a

危

KI, abu(nai), aya(ui) – dangerous

危険	kiken	danger	533
危機	kiki	crisis, critical moment	528
危急	kikyū	emergency, crisis	303
危害	kigai	injury, harm	518
危ぐ	kigu	fear, misgivings, apprehension	

危 危 危

危 危 危

| 535 | 扌 木 宀 |
| | 3c 4a 2i |

TAN, sagu(ru) – search/grope for; **saga(su)** – look for

探検/険	tanken	exploration, expedition	531, 533
探知	tanchi	detection	214
探り出す	saguridasu	spy/sniff out (a secret)	53
探し回る	sagashimawaru	look/search around for	90

探

| 536 | 氵 木 宀 |
| | 3a 4a 2i |

SHIN, fuka(i) – deep; **fuka(meru/maru)** – make/become deeper, more intense

深度	shindo	depth, deepness	377
深夜	shin'ya	dead of night, late at night	471
情け深い	nasakebukai	compassionate, merciful	209
興味深い	kyōmibukai	very interesting	368, 307

深

| 537 | 糸 氵 一 |
| | 6a 3a 1a3 |

RYOKU, [ROKU], midori – green

緑地	ryokuchi	green tract of land	118
新緑	shinryoku	fresh verdure/greenery	174
葉緑素	yōryokuso	chlorophyll	253, 271
緑青	rokushō	verdigris, green/copper rust	208
緑色	midoriiro	green, green-colored	204

緑

| 538 | 金 氵 一 |
| | 8a 3a 1a3 |

ROKU – record

記録	kiroku	record	371
録音	rokuon	(sound) recording	347
録画	rokuga	videotape recording	274
目録	mokuroku	catalog, inventory, list	55
付録	furoku	supplement, appendix, addendum	192

録

539 一 ノ
1a2 1c

YO, ata(eru) – give, grant

与党	*yotō*	party in power, government	495
関与	*kan'yo*	participation	398
給与	*kyūyo*	allowance, wage	346
供与	*kyōyo*	give, grant, furnish	197
賞与	*shōyo*	bonus	500

540 冖 一 ノ
2i 1a2 1c

SHA, utsu(su) – copy down; copy, duplicate; depict; photograph; **utsu(ru)** – be taken, turn out (photo)

写真	*shashin*	photograph	422
映写機	*eishaki*	projector	352, 528
写生	*shasei*	sketch, painting from nature	44
写実的	*shajitsuteki*	realistic, graphic	203, 210

541 十 土 一
(2k) 3b 1a

KŌ, kanga(eru) – think, consider

思考	*shikō*	thinking, thought	99
考案	*kōan*	conception, idea, design	106
考証	*kōshō*	historical research	484
考古学	*kōkogaku*	archaeology	172, 109
考え方	*kangaekata*	way of thinking, viewpoint	70

542 十 土 子
(2k) 3b 2c

KŌ – filial piety

(親)孝行	*(oya)kōkō*	filial piety, obedience to parents	175, 68
孝養	*kōyō*	discharge of filial duties	402
(親)不孝	*(oya)fukō*	undutifulness to one's parents	175, 94

543	耂 土 卜 (2k) 3b 2m	**RŌ, o(iru), fu(keru)** – grow old

老

老人	rōjin	old man/woman/people	1
長老	chōrō	elder, senior member	95
元老	genrō	genro; elder statesman	137
老夫婦	rōfūfu	old married couple	315, 316
老子	Rōshi	Laozi, Lao-tzu	103

老　老　老

老老老

544	艹 口 厂 3k 3d 2p	**JAKU, [NYAKU], waka(i)** – young; **mo(shikuwa)** – or

若

老若	rōnyaku, rōjaku	young and old, youth and age	543
若者	wakamono	young man/people	164
若手	wakate	young man, younger member	57
若人	wakōdo	young man, a youth	1
若死に	wakajini	die young	85

若　若　若

若若若

545	艹 口 十 3k 3d 2k	**KU, kuru(shimu)** – suffer; **kuru(shimeru)** – torment; **kuru(shii)** – painful; **niga(i)** – bitter; **niga(ru)** – scowl

苦

苦労	kurō	trouble, hardship, adversity	233
苦心	kushin	pains, efforts	97
病苦	byōku	the pain of illness	380
重苦しい	omokurushii	oppressed, gloomy, ponderous	227

苦　苦　苦

苦苦苦

546	車 月 亻 7c 4b 2a	**YU** – send, transport

輸

輸入	yunyū	import	52
輸出	yushutsu	export	53
輸送	yusō	transport	441
運輸	un'yu	transport, conveyance	439
空輸	kūyu	air transport, shipment by air	140

輸　輸　輸

輸輸輸

547

車 土 又
7c 3b 2h

KEI, karu(i), karo(yaka) – light

軽工業	keikōgyō	light industry	139, 279
軽食	keishoku	light meal	322
軽音楽	keiongaku	light music	347, 358
気軽	kigaru	lighthearted, cheerful, feel free (to)	134
手軽	tegaru	easy, light, simple, cheap	57

548

糸 土 又
6a 3b 2h

KEI – longitude; sutra; passage of time; **KYŌ** – sutra; **he(ru)** – pass, elapse

経験	keiken	experience	532
経歴	keireki	one's life history, career	480
経理	keiri	accounting	143
神経	shinkei	a nerve	310

549

氵 亠 一
3a 2j 1a2

SAI, su(mu) – come to an end; be paid; suffice; **su(masu)** – finish, settle; pay; make do, manage

経済	keizai	economy, economics	548
返済	hensai	payment, repayment	442
決済	kessai	settlement of accounts	356
使用済み	shiyōzumi	used up	331, 107

550

刂 亠 一
2f 2j 1a2

ZAI – medicine, dose

薬剤	yakuzai	medicine, drug	359
薬剤師	yakuzaishi	pharmacist, druggist	359, 409
調剤	chōzai	compounding/preparation of medicines	342
下剤	gezai	laxative	31
解毒剤	gedokuzai	antidote	474, 522

551　才　SAI – talent, genius

天才	*tensai*	a genius	141
才子	*saishi*	talented person	103
才能	*sainō*	talent, ability	386
多才	*tasai*	many-talented	229
十八才	*jūhassai*	18 years old	12, 10

552　材　ZAI – wood; material; talent

材料	*zairyō*	materials, ingredients	319
取材	*shuzai*	collection of material, news gathering	65
教材	*kyōzai*	teaching materials	245
題材	*daizai*	subject matter, theme	354
材木	*zaimoku*	wood, lumber	22

553　財　ZAI, [SAI] – money, wealth, property

財産	*zaisan*	estate, assets, property	278
財政	*zaisei*	finances, financial affairs	483
財務	*zaimu*	financial affairs	235
財界	*zaikai*	financial world, business circles	454
文化財	*bunkazai*	cultural asset	111, 254

554　因　IN – cause; yo(ru) – depend (on); be limited (to)

原因	*gen'in*	cause	136
主因	*shuin*	primary/main cause	155
死因	*shiin*	cause of death	85
要因	*yōin*	important factor, chief cause	419
因果	*inga*	cause and effect	487

555	心 口 イ 4k 3s 2a	**ON** – kindness, goodness; favor; gratitude

恩 恩 恩

恩給	onkyū	pension	346
恩賞	onshō	a reward	500
恩人	onjin	benefactor; patron	1
恩返し	ongaeshi	repayment of a favor	442
恩知らず	onshirazu	ingratitude; ingrate	214

556	氵 艹 口 3a 3k 3s	**KAN** – Han (Chinese dynasty), China; man, fellow

漢 漢 漢

漢字	kanji	Chinese character	110
漢文	kanbun	Chinese writing; Chinese classics	111
漢時代	kanjidai	Han dynasty/period	42, 256
好/悪漢	kō/ak-kan	nice fellow/scoundrel, villain	104, 304
門外漢	mongaikan	outsider, layman	161, 83

557	隹 艹 口 8c 3k 3s	**NAN, muzuka(shii), kata(i)** – difficult

難 難 難

難題	nandai	difficult problem/question	354
難病	nanbyō	incurable disease	380
難民	nanmin	refugees	177
海難	kainan	disaster at sea, shipwreck	117
非難	hinan	adverse criticism	498

558	口 木 3s 4a	**KON, koma(ru)** – be distressed

困 困 困

困難	konnan	difficulty, trouble	557
困苦	konku	hardships, adversity	545
困り果てる	komarihateru	be greatly troubled, nonplussed	487
困り切る	komarikiru	be in a bad fix, at a loss	39

559	力 艹 口 2g 3k 3s	**KIN, [GON], tsuto(meru)** – be employed; **tsuto(maru)** – be fit for			
		勤労	kinrō	work, labor	233
		勤務	kinmu	service, being on duty/at work	235
		通勤	tsūkin	going to work, commuting	150
		転勤	tenkin	be transferred (to another job)	433

勤

勤 勤 勤

勤 勤 勤

560	扌 厂 一 3c 2p 1a2	**TEI** – resist			
		抵当	teitō	mortgage, hypothec	77
		大抵	taitei	generally, for the most part, usually	26

抵

抵 抵 抵

抵 抵 抵

561	亻 厂 一 2a 2p 1a2	**TEI, hiku(i)** – low; **hiku(meru/maru)** – make/become lower			
		最低	saitei	lowest, minimum	263
		低地	teichi	low ground, lowlands	118
		低所得	teishotoku	low income	153, 374
		低成長	teiseichō	low growth	261, 95
		低能	teinō	weak intellect, mental deficiency	386

低

低 低 低

低 低 低

562	广 厂 一 3q 2p 1a2	**TEI, soko** – bottom			
		根底	kontei	base, foundation	314
		海底	kaitei	bottom of the sea, ocean floor	117
		河底	katei	bottom of a river, riverbed	389
		底力	sokojikara	latent energy/power	100
		底値	sokone	rock-bottom price	425

底

底 底 底

底 底 底

563	阝 厂 一 2d 2p 1a2	**TEI** – mansion, residence			

邸

公 邸	*kōtei*	official residence	126
官 邸	*kantei*	official residence	326
私 邸	*shitei*	one's private residence	125
邸 宅	*teitaku*	residence, mansion	178
邸 内	*teinai*	the grounds, the premises	84

564	夂 木 4i 4a	**JŌ** – article, clause; line, stripe			

条

条 約	*jōyaku*	treaty	211
条 文	*jōbun*	the text, provisions	111
第 一 条	*daiichijō*	Article 1 (in a law/contract/treaty)	404, 2
条 理	*jōri*	logic, reason	143
信 条	*shinjō*	a belief, article of faith	157

565	刂 土 亻 2f 3b 2a	**KEI, chigi(ru)** – pledge, vow, promise			

契

| 契 約 | *keiyaku* | contract | 211 |
| 契 機 | *keiki* | opportunity, chance | 528 |

566	ノ 厂 丶 (1c) 2p 1d	**SHI** – family, surname; Mr.; **uji** – family, lineage			

氏

氏 名	*shimei*	(full) name	82
坂 本 氏	*Sakamoto-shi*	Mr. Sakamoto	443, 25
同 氏	*dōshi*	the said person, he	198
両 氏	*ryōshi*	both (gentlemen)	200
氏 神	*ujigami*	tutelary deity, genius loci	310

567	女 日 厂	***KON*** – marriage		
	3e 4c 2p	結婚	*kekkon*	marriage	485

KON – marriage

結婚	*kekkon*	marriage	485
結婚式	*kekkonshiki*	marriage ceremony, wedding	485, 525
婚約	*kon'yaku*	engagement	211
未婚	*mikon*	unmarried	306
新婚旅行	*shinkon ryokō*	honeymoon	174, 222, 68

KYŪ – rank, class

進級	*shinkyū*	(school/military) promotion	437
高級	*kōkyū*	high rank; high class, de luxe	190
上級	*jōkyū*	upper grade, senior	32
学級	*gakkyū*	class in school	109
同級生	*dōkyūsei*	classmate	198, 44

TŌ – class, grade; equality; etc.; *hito(shii)* – equal

等級	*tōkyū*	class, grade, rank	568
一等	*ittō*	first class	2
平等	*byōdō*	equality	202
同等	*dōtō*	equality, same rank	198
高等学校	*kōtō gakkō*	senior high school	190, 109, 115

SHI – poetry, poem

詩人	*shijin*	poet	1
詩歌	*shiika, shika*	poetry	392
詩情	*shijō*	poetic sentiment	209
詩集	*shishū*	collection of poems	436
漢詩	*kanshi*	Chinese poem/poetry	556

571	亻2a 士3b 十2k	**JI, samurai** – samurai		
		侍者	*jisha*	attendant, valet, page	164
		侍女	*jijo*	lady-in-waiting, lady's attendant	102
		侍医	*jii*	court physician	220
		侍気質	*samurai katagi*	the samurai spirit	134, 176
		七人の侍	*Shichinin no Samurai*	(The Seven Samurai)	9, 1

侍　侍　侍

572	士3p	**SHI** – samurai, man, scholar		
		人間同士	*ningen dōshi*	fellow human being	1, 43, 198
		力士	*rikishi*	sumo wrestler	100
		代議士	*daigishi*	dietman, congressman, M.P.	256, 292
		学士	*gakushi*	university graduate	109
		税理士	*zeirishi*	(licensed) tax accountant	399, 143

士　士　士

573	士3p 心4k	**SHI, kokorozashi** – will, intention, aim; **kokoroza(su)** – intend, aim at, have in view		
		意志	*ishi*	will	132
		志向	*shikō*	intention, inclination	199
		同志	*dōshi*	like-minded (person)	198
		有志	*yūshi*	voluntary; those interested	265

志　志　志

574	言7a 心4k 士3p	**SHI** – write down, chronicle; magazine		
		誌上	*shijō*	in a magazine	32
		誌面	*shimen*	page of a magazine	274
		日誌	*nisshi*	diary	5
		地誌	*chishi*	a topography, geographical description	118
		書誌学	*shoshigaku*	bibliography	131, 109

誌　誌　誌

575	隹 木 一
	8c 4a 1a

ZATSU, ZŌ – miscellany, a mix

雑誌	zasshi	magazine	574
雑音	zatsuon	noise, static	347
雑感	zakkan	miscellaneous thoughts/impressions	262
雑草	zassō	weeds	249
雑木林	zōkibayashi	thicket of assorted trees	22, 127

576	木 几 又
	4a 2s 2h

SATSU, [SAI], [SETSU], koro(su) – kill

自殺	jisatsu	suicide	62
暗殺	ansatsu	assassination	348
毒殺	dokusatsu	killing by poison	522
殺人	satsujin	a murder	1
人殺し	hitogoroshi	murder, murderer	1

577	言 几 又
	7a 2s 2h

SETSU, mō(keru) – establish, set up, prepare

設立	setsuritsu	establishment, founding	121
設置	setchi	establishment, founding, institution	426
設定	settei	establishment, creation	355
新設	shinsetsu	newly established/organized	174
私設	shisetsu	private	125

578	亻 口 卩
	2a 3d 2e

MEI – command; fate; life; **MYŌ, inochi** – life

生命 (保険)	seimei (hoken)	life (insurance)	44, 489, 533
運命	unmei	fate	439
使命	shimei	mission, errand	331
短命	tanmei	a short life	215
任命	ninmei	appointment, nomination	334

579

亻 心 一
2a 4k 1a2

念

NEN – thought, idea; desire; concern, attention

記念日	kinenbi	memorial day, anniversary	371, 5
記念切手	kinen kitte	commemorative stamp	371, 39, 57
理念	rinen	idea, doctrine, ideology	143
信念	shinnen	belief, faith, conviction	157
念入り	nen'iri	careful, scrupulous, thorough	52

580

氵日 ⺌
3a 4c 3n

源

GEN, minamoto – source, origin

起源	kigen	origin	373
根源	kongen	origin	314
財源	zaigen	source of revenue	553
源平	Gen-Pei	Genji and Heike clans	202
源氏物語	Genji Monogatari	(The Tale of Genji)	566, 79, 67

581

頁日 ⺌
9a 4c 3n

願

GAN, nega(u) – petition, request, desire

大願	taigan	great ambition, earnest wish	26
念願	nengan	one's heart's desire	579
出願	shutsugan	application	53
願書	gansho	written request, application	131
志願	shigan	application, volunteering, desire	573

582

扌ノ 丶
3c 1c 1d

払

FUTSU, hara(u) – pay; sweep away

払底	futtei	shortage, scarcity	562
支払い	shiharai	payment	318
前払い	maebarai	payment in advance	47
現金払い	genkinbarai	cash payment	298, 23
分割払い	bunkatsubarai	payment in installments	38, 519

583	イ ノ ヽ 2a 1c 1d	**BUTSU, hotoke** – Buddha		
		仏教 bukkyō Buddhism	245	
		大仏 daibutsu great statue of Buddha	26	
		石仏 sekibutsu stone image of Buddha	78	
		念仏 nenbutsu Buddhist prayer	579	
		日仏 Nichi-Futsu Japanese-French	5	

仏

584	十一 2k 1a	**KAN, hi(ru)** – get dry; **ho(su)** – dry; drink up		
		(潮の)干満 (shio no) kanman tide, ebb and flow	467, 201	
		干潮 kanchō ebb/low tide	467	
		干渉 kanshō interfere, meddle	432	
		若干 jakkan some, a number of	544	
		物干し monohoshi frame for drying clothes	79	

干

585	リ十一 2f 2k 1a	**KAN** – publish		
		週刊(誌) shūkan(shi) weekly magazine	92, 574	
		日刊紙 nikkanshi daily newspaper	5, 180	
		夕刊 yūkan evening newspaper/edition	81	
		新刊 shinkan new publication	174	
		未刊行 mikankō unpublished	306, 68	

刊

586	山厂十 3o 2p 2k	**GAN, kishi** – bank, shore, coast		
		西岸 seigan west bank/coast	72	
		対岸 taigan opposite shore	365	
		海岸 kaigan seashore, coast	117	
		河岸 kawagishi, kagan riverbank	389	
		川岸 kawagishi riverbank	33	

岸

587	日 卜 ノ 4c 2m2 1c	**KAI, mina** – all			
		皆済	kaisai	payment in full	549
		皆勤	kaikin	perfect attendance (at work/school)	559
		皆さん	minasan	everybody; Ladies and Gentlemen!	
		皆目	kaimoku	utterly; (not) at all	55
		皆無	kaimu	nothing/none at all	93

皆

588	阝 日 卜 2d 4c 2m2	**KAI** – stair, story, level			
		三階	sangai, sankai	third floor	4
		階段	kaidan	stairs, stairway	362
		段階	dankai	stage, phase	362
		階級	kaikyū	social class	568
		音階	onkai	musical scale	347

階

589	阝 土 卜 2d 3b 2m2	**HEI** – steps (of the throne)			
		天皇陛下	tennō-heika	H.M. the Emperor	141, 297, 31
		国王陛下	kokuō-heika	H.M. the King	40, 294, 31
		女王陛下	joō-heika	H.M. the Queen	102, 294, 31
		両陛下	ryōheika	Their Majesties the Emperor and Empress	200, 31

陛

590	冫 一 2b2 1a2	**U, ha, hane** – feather, wing			
		羽毛	umō	feather, plumage	287
		白羽	shiraha	white feather	205
		羽音	haoto	flapping of wings	347
		一羽	ichiwa	1 bird	2
		羽田	Haneda	(airport in Tokyo)	35

羽

591	日 冫 一 4c 2b2 1a2	**SHŪ**, *nara(u)* – learn			
		学習	gakushū	learning, study	109
		独習	dokushū	self-study	219
		予習	yoshū	preparation of lessons	393
		常習	jōshū	custom; habit	497
		習字	shūji	penmanship, calligraphy	110

習

592	立 冫 一 5b 2b2 1a2	**YOKU** – the next, following			
		翌朝	yokuasa, yokuchō	the next morning	469
		翌日	yokujitsu	the next/following day	5
		翌週	yokushū	the following week, the week after that	92
		翌年	yokunen	the following year	45
		翌々日	yokuyokujitsu	2 days later/thereafter	5

翌

593	言 火 7a 4d2	**DAN** – conversation			
		会談	kaidan	a conversation, conference	158
		対談	taidan	face-to-face talk, conversation	365
		談話	danwa	conversation	238
		相談	sōdan	consultation	146
		下相談	shitasōdan	preliminary negotiations	31, 146

談

594	言 尸 、 7a 3r 1d	**YAKU** – translation; *wake* – reason; meaning; circumstances			
		通訳	tsūyaku	interpreting, interpreter	150
		英訳	eiyaku	a translation into English	353
		全訳	zen'yaku	a complete translation	89
		訳者	yakusha	translator	164
		言い訳	iiwake	apology; excuse	66

訳

595 釈 (6b 3r 1d)

SHAKU – explanation

解釈	kaishaku	interpretation, construal	474
釈明	shakumei	explanation, vindication	18
釈放	shakuhō	release, discharge	512
保釈	hoshaku	(prison) bail	489
注釈	chūshaku	comments, annotation	357

596 翻 (6b 5f 2b2)

HON, hirugae(su) – (tr.) turn over; change (one's opinion); wave (a flag); **hirugae(ru)** – (intr.) turn over; wave

翻訳	hon'yaku	translation, translate	594
翻案	hon'an	an adaptation	106
翻意	hon'i	change one's mind	132
翻ろう	honrō	trifle with, make sport of	

597 橋 (4a 3d2)

KYŌ, hashi – bridge

歩道橋	hodōkyō	pedestrian bridge	431, 149
鉄橋	tekkyō	iron bridge; railway bridge	312
石橋	ishibashi	stone bridge	78
つり橋	tsuribashi	suspension bridge	
日本橋	Nihonbashi	(area of Tokyo)	5, 25

598 柱 (4a 4f 1d)

CHŪ, hashira – pillar, column, pole

支柱	shichū	prop, support, strut	318
電柱	denchū	utility/electric pole	108
水銀柱	suiginchū	column of mercury	21, 313
円柱	enchū	column, cylinder	13
大黒柱	daikokubashira	central pillar, mainstay	26, 206

599	馬 王 丶 10a 4f 1d	**CHŪ** – stop; reside		
		駐車場 chūshajō parking lot		133, 154
		駐在 chūzai stay, residence		268
		駐日 chūnichi resident/stationed in Japan		5
		進駐 shinchū stationing, occupation		437

駐

600	一 日 十 (1a) 4c 2k2	**SEN, moppa(ra)** – entirely, exclusively		
		専門家 senmonka specialist, expert		161, 165
		専任 sennin exclusive duty, full-time		334
		専制 sensei absolutism, despotism		427
		専売 senbai monopoly		239
		専用 (駐車場) sen'yō (chūshajō) private (parking lot)		107, 599, 133, 154

専

601	十 日 丶 2k3 4c 1d2	**HAKU, [BAKU]** – extensive, broad, many		
		博物館 hakubutsukan museum		79, 327
		博学 hakugaku broad knowledge, erudition		109
		博士 hakase, hakushi doctor		572
		博愛 hakuai philanthropy		259
		万博 banpaku international exhibition		16

博

602	扌 ⺌ 冖 3c 3n 2i	**JU, sazu(keru)** – grant, teach; **sazu(karu)** – be granted, taught		
		授業 jugyō teaching, instruction		279
		教授 kyōju instruction; professor		245
		授受 juju giving and receiving, transfer		260
		授与 juyo conferment, presentation		539
		授賞 jushō receiving a prize		500

授

603

石 隹 宀
5a 8c 2i

KAKU, tashi(ka) – certain; ***tashi(kameru)*** – make sure of, verify

確立	kakuritsu	establishment, settlement	121
確定	kakutei	decision, settlement	355
確実	kakujitsu	certain, reliable	203
確信	kakushin	firm belief, conviction	157
正確	seikaku	accurate, precise, correct	275

604

目 隹 ⺍
5c 8c 2o

KAN – appearance, view

観光	kankō	sight-seeing, tourism	138
外観	gaikan	(external) appearance	83
主観的	shukanteki	subjective	155, 210
楽観的	rakkanteki	optimistic	358, 210
観念	kannen	idea; sense (of duty/justice)	579

605

⺍ 目 宀
3n 5c 2i

KAKU, obo(eru) – remember, bear in mind, learn; feel; ***sa(meru/masu)*** – (intr./tr.) awake, wake up

感覚	kankaku	sense, sensation, feeling	262
直覚	chokkaku	intuition, insight	423
見覚え	mioboe	recognition, knowing by sight	63
目覚まし (時計)	mezamashi(-dokei)	alarm clock	55, 42, 340

606

ネ 目 ⺀
4e 5c 2o

SHI – seeing, regarding as

視力	shiryoku	visual acuity, eyesight	100
近視	kinshi	nearsightedness, shortsightedness	445
重視	jūshi	attach importance to, stress	227
無視	mushi	ignore, disregard	93
視界	shikai	field of vision	454

607	目 亻 丶 5c 2a 2o	**KI** – standard, measure			
		規定	*kitei*	stipulations, provisions, regulations	355
		定規	*jōgi*	ruler, square; standard, norm	355
		正規	*seiki*	regular, formal, regulation	275
		新規	*shinki*	new	174
		法規	*hōki*	laws and regulations, legislation	123

608	貝 刂 7b 2f	**SOKU** – rule, law			
		規則	*kisoku*	rule, regulation	607
		原則	*gensoku*	general rule, principle	136
		法則	*hōsoku*	a law	123
		変則	*hensoku*	irregularity, anomaly	257
		会則	*kaisoku*	rules of an association	158

609	亻 貝 刂 2a 7b 2f	**SOKU, kawa** – side			
		側面	*sokumen*	side, flank	274
		側近者	*sokkinsha*	one's close associates	445, 164
		左側	*hidarigawa*	left side	75
		反対側	*hantaigawa*	opposite side	324, 365
		日本側	*Nippongawa, Nihongawa*	the Japanese side	5, 25

610	氵 貝 刂 3a 7b 2f	**SOKU, haka(ru)** – measure			
		測量	*sokuryō*	measurement, surveying	411
		測定	*sokutei*	measuring	355
		観測	*kansoku*	observation	604
		目測	*mokusoku*	measurement by eye, estimation	55
		予測	*yosoku*	estimate, forecast	393

611 列

リ ケ 一
2f 2n 1a

RETSU – row

列車	*ressha*	train	133
列島	*rettō*	chain of islands, archipelago	286
列国	*rekkoku*	world powers, nations	40
行列	*gyōretsu*	queue; procession; matrix	68
後列	*kōretsu*	back row	48

612 例

イ ケ リ
2a 2n 2f

REI – example; custom, precedent; **tato(eru)** – compare

例外	*reigai*	exception	83
特例	*tokurei*	special case, exception	282
先例	*senrei*	previous example, precedent	50
例年	*reinen*	normal year; every year	45
条例	*jōrei*	regulations, ordinance	564

613 完

宀 ソ 一
3m 2o 1a2

KAN – completion

完結	*kanketsu*	completion	485
完全	*kanzen*	complete, perfect	89
完成	*kansei*	completion, accomplishment	261
未完成	*mikansei*	incomplete, unfinished	306, 261
完敗	*kanpai*	complete defeat	511

614 院

阝 宀 ソ
2d 3m 2o

IN – institution

病院	*byōin*	hospital	380
入院	*nyūin*	admission to a hospital	52
大学院	*daigakuin*	graduate school	26, 109
養老院	*yōrōin*	old folks' home	402, 543
両院	*ryōin*	both houses (of the Diet/Congress/Parliament)	200

615	ネ 4e	**JI, SHI, shime(su)** – show			
		公示	*kōji*	public announcement	126
		明示	*meiji*	clear statement	18
		教示	*kyōji*	instruction, teaching	245
		暗示	*anji*	hint, suggestion	348
		示談	*jidan*	out-of-court settlement	593

示 示 示 示

616	宀 ネ 3m 4e	**SHŪ, SŌ** – religion, sect			
		宗教	*shūkyō*	religion	245
		宗門	*shūmon*	sect	161
		宗徒	*shūto*	adherent, believer	430
		改宗	*kaishū*	conversion, become a convert	514
		宗家	*sōke*	the head family	165

宗 宗 宗 宗

617	ネ ケ 又 4e 2n 2h	**SAI, matsu(ru)** – deify, worship; *matsu(ri)* – festival			
		祭日	*saijitsu*	holiday; festival day	5
		百年祭	*hyakunensai*	centennial	14, 45
		文化祭	*bunkasai*	cultural festival	111, 254
		秋祭り	*akimatsuri*	autumn festival	462
		後の祭り	*ato no matsuri*	Too late!	48

祭 祭 祭 祭

618	阝 ネ ケ 2d 4e 2n	**SAI** – time, occasion; *kiwa* – side, brink, edge			
		国際	*kokusai*	international	40
		交際	*kōsai*	association, company, acquaintance	114
		実際	*jissai*	truth, reality, actual practice	203
		水際	*mizugiwa*	water's edge, shore	21
		際立つ	*kiwadatsu*	be conspicuous, stand out	121

際 際 際 際

619	宀 ネ ク 3m 4e 2n	**SATSU** – surmise, judge, understand, sympathize	
		観 察 *kansatsu* observation	604
		検 察 *kensatsu* criminal investigation, prosecution	531
		視 察 *shisatsu* inspection, observation	606
		考 察 *kōsatsu* consideration, examination	541
		明 察 *meisatsu* discernment, keen insight	18

察

620	ネ | 4e 1b	**REI, RAI** – courtesy; salutation; gratitude, remuneration	
		祭 礼 *sairei* religious festival	617
		礼 式 *reishiki* etiquette	525
		失 礼 *shitsurei* rudeness	311
		非 礼 *hirei* impoliteness	498
		無 礼 *burei* rudeness, impertinence, affront	93

礼

621	ネ 厂 一 4e 2p 1a	**KI, ino(ru)** – pray	
		祈 念 *kinen* a prayer	579
		祈 願 *kigan* a prayer	581
		祈 とう (書) *kitō(sho)* prayer (book)	131
		祈 り *inori* a prayer	
		主 の 祈 り *shu no inori* the Lord's Prayer	155

祈

622	ネ 冂 一 4e 2r 1a3	**SO** – ancestor	
		祖 先 *sosen* ancestor, forefather	50
		祖 母/父 *sobo/fu* grandmother/father	112, 113
		祖 国 *sokoku* one's homeland/fatherland	40
		元 祖 *ganso* originator, founder, inventor	137
		宗 祖 *shūso* founder of a sect	616

祖

623	力 冂 一 2g 2r 1a2	**JO**, *tasu(keru)* – help, rescue; *tasu(karu)* – be helped, rescued; *suke* – assistance		
		助力	*joryoku*	help, assistance	100
		助言	*jogen*	advice	66
		助手	*joshu*	helper, assistant	57
		助け合う	*tasukeau*	help each other	159

助

助　助　助

助　助　助

624	木 冂 一 4a 2r 1a3	**SA** – investigate		
		調査	*chōsa*	investigation, inquiry, observation	342
		検査	*kensa*	inspection, examination	531
		査問	*samon*	inquiry, hearing	162
		査察	*sasatsu*	inspection, observation	619
		査定	*satei*	assessment	355

査

査　査　査

査　査　査

625	宀 日 一 3m 4c 1a2	**SEN** – announce		
		宣言	*sengen*	declaration, manifesto	66
		独立宣言	*dokuritsu sengen*	declaration of independence	219, 121, 66
		宣伝	*senden*	propaganda; advertising, publicity	434
		宣戦	*sensen*	declaration of war	301
		宣教師	*senkyōshi*	a missionary	245, 409

宣

宣　宣　宣

宣　宣　宣

626	冫 犭 丨 2b 3g 1b	**JŌ** – condition, circumstances; form; letter		
		状態	*jōtai*	circumstances, situation	387
		現状	*genjō*	present situation	298
		白状	*hakujō*	confession	205
		礼状	*reijō*	letter of thanks	620
		招待状	*shōtaijō*	written invitation	455, 452

状

状　状　状

状　状　状

627

将
2b 3n 2k

SHŌ – commander, general; soon

将来	*shōrai*	future	69
将軍	*shōgun*	shogun, general	438
大将	*taishō*	general, leader	26
主将	*shushō*	(team) captain	155
将校	*shōkō*	officer	115

628

提
3c 4c 2m

TEI – present, submit; *sa(geru)* – carry (in the hand)

提案	*teian*	proposition, proposal	106
提供	*teikyō*	offer	197
提議	*teigi*	proposal, suggestion	292
提出	*teishutsu*	presentation, filing	53
前提	*zentei*	premise	47

629

太
1a 2a 1d

TAI, TA, *futo(i)* – fat, thick; *futo(ru)* – get fat/thick

太平洋	*Taiheiyō*	Pacific Ocean	202, 289
皇太子	*kōtaishi*	crown prince	297, 103
太古	*taiko*	ancient times, antiquity	172
太字	*futoji*	thick character, boldface	110
太刀	*tachi*	(long) sword	37

630

陽
2d 4c 1a2

YŌ – positive, male; sun

太陽	*taiyō*	sun	629
陽光	*yōkō*	sunshine, sunlight	138
陽気	*yōki*	season, weather; cheerfulness, gaiety	134
陽性	*yōsei*	positive	98
陽子	*yōshi*	proton	103

631	扌 日 一 3c 4c 1a2	YŌ, a(geru) – raise; fry; a(garu) – rise		
		高揚	kōyō	uplift, surge	190
		揚水車	yōsuisha	scoop wheel	21, 133
		意気揚々	ikiyōyō	triumphantly, exultantly	132, 134
		荷揚げ	niage	unloading, discharge, landing	391
		引き揚げ	hikiage	withdrawal, evacuation	216

揚　揚　揚

揚　揚　揚

632	氵 日 一 3a 4c 1a2	TŌ, yu – hot water		
		湯治	tōji	hot-spring cure	493
		湯元	yumoto	source of a hot spring	137
		湯ぶね	yubune	bathtub	
		茶の湯	cha no yu	tea ceremony	251
		湯上がり	yuagari	just after a bath	32

湯　湯　湯

湯　湯　湯

633	亻 日 一 2a 4c 1a3	SHŌ, kizu – wound, injury; ita(mu) – hurt; ita(meru) – injure		
		負傷	fushō	wound, injury	510
		傷害	shōgai	injury, damage	518
		重/軽傷	jū/keishō	severe/minor injuries	227, 547
		死傷者	shishōsha	the killed and injured, casualties	85, 164
		中傷	chūshō	slander	28

傷　傷　傷

傷　傷　傷

634	氵 皿 日 3a 5h 4c	ON, atata(kai/ka) – warm; atata(maru/meru) – (intr./tr.) warm up		
		温度	ondo	temperature	377
		気/水/体温	ki/sui/tai-on	air/water/body temperature	134, 21, 61
		温室	onshitsu	hothouse, greenhouse	166
		温和	onwa	mild, gentle	124

温　温　温

温　温　温

635	日 ⸚ 厂 4c 3n 2p	**DAN, atata(kai/ka)** – warm; **atata(maru/meru)** – (intr./tr.) warm up

暖　　寒暖計　　　*kandankei*　　thermometer　　　　　　　　457, 340
温暖　　*ondan*　　warm　　　　　　　　　　634
暖流　　*danryū*　　warm ocean current　　　　247
暖冬　　*dantō*　　warm/mild winter　　　　459

636	雨 一 ノ 8d 1a2 1c	**UN, kumo** – cloud

雲　　風雲　　　*fūun*　　　wind and clouds; situation　　　　29
暗雲　　*an'un*　　dark clouds　　　　　348
雨雲　　*amagumo*　　rain cloud　　　　　30
入道雲　　*nyūdōgumo*　　cumulonimbus, thunderhead　　52, 149
出雲大社　*Izumo Taisha*　　Izumo Shrine　　　53, 26, 308

637	日 雨 一 4c 8d 1a2	**DON, kumo(ru)** – cloud up, get cloudy

曇天　　*donten*　　cloudy/overcast sky　　　　141
花曇り　　*hanagumori*　　cloudy weather in cherryblossom season　255
曇りがち　*kumorigachi*　　broken clouds, mostly cloudy
曇りガラス　*kumorigarasu*　　ground/frosted/mat glass

638	日 土 ノ 4c2 3b 1c	**SHO, atsu(i)** – hot (weather)

暑　　寒暑　　　*kansho*　　cold and heat　　　　457
暑気　　*shoki*　　the heat　　　　　134
暑中　　*shochū*　　middle of summer　　　28
大暑　　*taisho*　　Japanese Midsummer Day (about July 24)　26
暑苦しい　*atsukurushii*　oppressively hot, sultry　　545

639	厂 日 子 2p 4c 2c

KŌ, atsu(i) – thick; kind, cordial

厚意	kōi	kind intentions, kindness	132
厚顔	kōgan	impudence, effrontery	277
厚生省	Kōseishō	Ministry of Health and Welfare	44, 145
厚相	kōshō	minister of health and welfare	146
厚紙	atsugami	thick paper, cardboard	180

640	宀 日 女 3m 4c 3e

EN – feast, banquet

宴会	enkai	dinner party, banquet	158
宴席	enseki	(one's seat in) a banquet hall	379
酒宴	shuen	feast, drinking bout	517
きょう宴	kyōen	banquet, feast, dinner	

641	宀 夂 口 3m 4i 3d

KYAKU, KAKU – guest, customer

客間/室	kyaku-ma/shitsu	guest room	43, 166
客船	kyakusen	passenger ship	376
乗客	jōkyaku	passenger	523
旅客	ryokaku	passenger, traveler	222
客観的	kyakkanteki	objective	604, 210

642	夂 口 4i 3d

KAKU, onoono – each, every; various

各地	kakuchi	every area; various places	118
各国	kakkoku	all/various countries	40
各種	kakushu	every kind, various types	228
各人	kakujin	each person, everyone	1
各自	kakuji	each person, everyone	62

643	木 夊 口 4a 4i 3d	**KAKU, [KŌ]** – status, rank; standard, rule; case	
		人格　　*jinkaku*　　personality, character	1
		性格　　*seikaku*　　character, personality	98
		価格　　*kakaku*　　price; value	421
		合格　　*gōkaku*　　pass (an exam)	159
		格子　　*kōshi*　　lattice, bars, grating, grille	103

格

644	一 丨 丶 1a 1b 1d	**GAN, maru(i)** – round; **maru(meru)** – make round, form into a ball; **-maru** – (suffix for names of ships)	
		丸薬　　　　*gan'yaku*　　pill	359
		丸太小屋　*marutagoya*　log cabin	629, 27, 167
		日本丸　　*Nihonmaru*　the ship *Nihon*	5, 25
		日の丸　　*Hi no Maru*　(Japanese) Rising-Sun Flag	5

丸

645	火 土 灬 4d 3b2 2o	**NETSU** – heat, fever; **atsu(i)** – hot (food)	
		熱病　　*netsubyō*　　fever	380
		高熱　　*kōnetsu*　　high fever	190
		熱湯　　*nettō*　　boiling water	632
		情熱　　*jōnetsu*　　passion	209
		熱心　　*nesshin*　　enthusiasm, zeal	97

熱

646	力 土 灬 2g 3b2 2o	**SEI, ikio(i)** – force, energy, vigor; trend	
		勢力　　*seiryoku*　　influence, force	100
		国勢　　*kokusei*　　state/condition of a country	40
		情勢　　*jōsei*　　the situation	209
		大勢　　*taisei*　　general situation/trend	26
		ōzei　　many people, large crowd	

勢

647	阝 土 丷 2d 3b2 2o	**RIKU** – land			
		大 陸	*tairiku*	continent, mainland	26
		陸 上	*rikujō*	land, ground	32
		上 陸	*jōriku*	landing, going ashore	32
		陸 路	*rikuro*	land route	151
		陸 軍	*rikugun*	army	438

陸

648	金 戈 一 8a 4n 1a2	**SEN** – money; 1/100 yen; **zeni** – money			
		金 銭	*kinsen*	money	23
		口 銭	*kōsen*	commission, percentage	54
		悪 銭	*akusen*	ill-gotten money	304
		銭 湯	*sentō*	public bath	632
		小 銭	*kozeni*	small change	27

銭

649	氵 戈 一 3a 4n 1a2	**SEN, asa(i)** – shallow			
		浅 海	*senkai*	shallow sea	117
		浅 見	*senken*	superficial view	63
		浅 学	*sengaku*	superficial knowledge	109
		浅 黒 い	*asaguroi*	dark-colored, swarthy	206
		遠 浅	*tōasa*	shoaling beach	446

浅

650	一 戈 夕 1a3 4n 2n	**ZAN, noko(su/ru)** – leave/remain behind			
		残 念	*zannen*	regret, disappointment, too bad	579
		残 業	*zangyō*	overtime	279
		残 高	*zandaka*	balance, remainder	190
		残 り 物	*nokorimono*	leftovers	79
		生 き 残 る	*ikinokoru*	survive	44

残

651

火 犭 丶
4d 3g 2n

ZEN, NEN – as, like

全 然	zenzen	(not) at all; completely	89
当 然	tōzen	naturally, (as a matter) of course	77
必 然	hitsuzen	inevitability, necessity	520
自 然	shizen	nature	62
天 然	tennen	natural	141

然

652

火 犭 丶
4d2 3g 2n

NEN, mo(eru) – (intr.) burn; **mo(yasu/su)** – (tr.) burn

燃 料	nenryō	fuel	319
不 燃 性	funensei	nonflammable, fireproof	94, 98
可 燃 性	kanensei	flammable, combustible	388, 98
内 燃 機 関	nainen kikan	internal-combustion engine	84, 528, 398
燃 え 上 が る	moeagaru	blaze up, burst into flames	32

燃

653

丶 口 イ
2o 3d 2a

KOKU, tani – valley

谷 間	tanima	valley	43
谷 底	tanisoko	bottom of a ravine/gorge	562
谷 川	tanigawa	mountain stream	33
長 谷 川	Hasegawa	(surname)	95, 33
四 ツ 谷	Yotsuya	(area of Tokyo)	6

谷

654

宀 口 丶
3m 3d 2o

YŌ – form, appearance; content

美 容 院	biyōin	beauty parlor, hairdresser's	401, 614
形 容	keiyō	form; metaphor	395
内 容	naiyō	content	84
容 器	yōki	container	527
容 量	yōryō	capacity, volume	411

容

655	貝 土 一 7b 3b 1a	***SEKI**, se(meru)* – condemn, censure; torture	
		責任	*sekinin*	responsibility	334
		重責	*jūseki*	heavy responsibility	227
		責務	*sekimu*	duty, obligation	235
		自責	*jiseki*	self-reproach, pangs of conscience	62
		引責	*inseki*	assume responsibility	216

656	禾 貝 土 5d 7b 3b	***SEKI**, tsu(mu)* – heap up, load; *tsu(moru)* – be piled up, accumulate; *tsu(mori)* – intention; estimate	
		面積	*menseki*	(surface) area	274
		積極的	*sekkyokuteki*	positive, active	336, 210
		積み重ねる	*tsumikasaneru*	stack up one on another	227
		見積(書)	*mitsumori(sho)*	(written) estimate	63, 131

657	＞ 目 王 2o 5c 4f	***CHAKU**, [JAKU]* – arrival; clothing; *ki(ru), tsu(keru)* – put on, wear; *ki(seru)* – dress (someone); *tsu(ku)* – arrive	
		着陸	*chakuriku*	(airplane) landing	647
		決着	*ketchaku*	conclusion, settlement, decision	356
		着物	*kimono*	kimono; clothing	79
		下着	*shitagi*	underwear	31

658	＞ 王 一 2o 4f 1a2	***SA*** – difference; *sa(su)* – hold (an umbrella); wear (a sword); offer (a cup of saké); thrust	
		時差	*jisa*	time difference/lag	42
		差別	*sabetsu*	discrimination	267
		交差点	*kōsaten*	intersection	114, 169
		差し支え	*sashitsukae*	impediment; objection	318

659	米 6b 月 4b 土 3b	**SEI, [SHŌ]** – spirit; energy, vitality

精

精力	seiryoku	energy, vigor, vitality	100
精神	seishin	mind, spirit	310
精液	seieki	semen, sperm	472
精進	shōjin	diligence, devotion; purification	437
不/無精	bushō	sloth, laziness, indolence	94, 93

660	氵 3a 月 4b 土 3b	**SEI, [SHŌ], kiyo(i)** – pure, clean, clear; **kiyo(meru)** – purify, cleanse; **kiyo(maru)** – be purified, cleansed

清

清酒	seishu	refined saké	517
清書	seisho	fair/clean copy	131
清水	seisui, shimizu	pure/clear water	21
	Kiyomizu	(temple in Kyoto)	

661	言 7a 月 4b 土 3b	**SEI, SHIN, ko(u)** – ask for; **u(keru)** – receive

請

請願	seigan	petition, application	581
要請	yōsei	demand, requirement, request	419
申請	shinsei	application, petition	309
強請	kyōsei	importunate demand; extortion	217
下請け	shitauke	subcontract	31

662	日 4c 月 4b 土 3b	**SEI, ha(reru/rasu)** – (intr./tr.) clear up

晴

晴天	seiten	clear sky, fine weather	141
晴曇	seidon	changeable, fair to cloudy	637
秋晴れ	akibare	clear autumn weather	462
見晴らし	miharashi	view, vista	63
気晴らし	kibarashi	pastime, diversion	134

| 663 | 月 4b | 圭 3b | 爫 2n | *SEI, [JŌ], shizu, shizu(ka)* – quiet, peaceful, still; *shizu(meru/maru)* – make/become peaceful |

静 物	seibutsu	still life	79
静 止	seishi	stillness, rest, stationary	477
安 静	ansei	rest, quiet, repose	105
平 静	heisei	calm, serenity	202

| 664 | 氵 3a | 爫 2n | 十 2k | *JŌ* – pure |

清 浄	seijō	purity, cleanliness	660
浄 化	jōka	purification	254
不 浄	fujō	dirtiness, impurity	94
浄 土 宗	Jōdoshū	the Jodo sect (of Buddhism)	24, 616

| 665 | 石 5a | 厂 2p | 又 2h | *HA, yabu(ru)* – tear, break; *yabu(reru)* – get torn/broken |

破 産	hasan	bankruptcy	278
破 局	hakyoku	catastrophe, ruin	170
破 約	hayaku	breach of contract/promise	211
破 れ 目	yabureme	a tear, split	55
見 破 る	miyaburu	see through	63

| 666 | 氵 3a | 厂 2p | 又 2h | *HA, nami* – wave |

波 止 場	hatoba	wharf, pier	477, 154
電 波	denpa	electric/radio wave	108
短 波	tanpa	shortwave	215
波 長	hachō	wavelength	95
波 乗 り	naminori	surfing	523

667	彳 3i	十 2k	一 1a4	**RITSU, [RICHI]** – law, regulation		

法律	hōritsu	law	123
規律	kiritsu	order, discipline, regulations	607
不文律	fubunritsu	unwritten law	94, 111
韻律	inritsu	rhythm, meter	349
自律神経	jiritsu shinkei	autonomic nerve	62, 310, 548

668	氵 3a	十 2k	一 1a4	**SHIN, tsu** – harbor, ferry		

津波	tsunami	tsunami, "tidal" wave	666
興味津々	kyōmi-shinshin	very interesting	368, 307
津軽半島	Tsugaru Hantō	Tsugaru Peninsula	547, 88, 286

669	氵 3a	艹 3k	ソ 2o	**KŌ, minato** – harbor, port		

空港	kūkō	airport	140
商/軍港	shō/gunkō	trading/naval port	412, 438
内港	naikō	inner harbor	84
港内	kōnai	in the harbor	84
港町	minatomachi	port city	182

670	氵 3a	弓 3h	宀 2j	**WAN** – bay		

東京湾	Tōkyō-wan	Tokyo Bay	71, 189
湾曲	wankyoku	curvature, bend	366
港湾	kōwan	harbor	669
港湾労働者	kōwan rōdōsha	port laborer, longshoreman	669, 233, 232, 164
台湾	Taiwan	Taiwan	492

671	女 十 一 3e 2k 1a3	**SAI, tsuma** – wife

夫妻	*fusai*	husband and wife, Mr. and Mrs.	315
妻子	*saishi*	wife and child/children, family	103
後妻	*gosai*	second wife	48
良妻	*ryōsai*	good wife	321
老妻	*rōsai*	one's aged wife	543

672	亠 丨 2j 1b	**BŌ, [MŌ]** – die; **na(i)** – dead, deceased

死亡者	*shibōsha*	the dead	85, 164
亡父	*bōfu*	one's late father	113
亡夫	*bōfu*	one's late husband	315
未亡人	*mibōjin*	widow	306, 1
亡命	*bōmei*	fleeing one's country, going into exile	578

673	王 月 亠 4f 4b 2j	**BŌ, MŌ, nozo(mu)** – desire, wish, hope for

志望	*shibō*	wish, aspiration	573
宿望	*shukubō*	long-cherished desire	179
要望	*yōbō*	demand, wish	419
失望	*shitsubō*	despair, disappointment	311
大望	*taibō*	great desire, ambition	26

674	王 耳 口 4f 6e 3d	**SEI** – holy

聖人	*seijin*	sage, holy man	1
神聖	*shinsei*	sacredness, sanctity	310
聖書	*seisho*	the Bible	131
聖堂	*seidō*	Confucian temple; church	496
聖母	*seibo*	the Holy Mother, the Blessed Mary	112

675 巾 厂 3f 2p

FU – spread; cloth; **nuno** – a cloth

財布	saifu	purse, wallet	553
毛布	mōfu	a blanket	287
分布	bunpu	distribution, range	38
配布	haifu	distribution, distributing widely	515
公布	kōfu	official announcement, promulgation	126

676 巾 厂 ノ 3f 2p 1c

KI – hope, desire; rarity, scarcity

希望	kibō	wish, hope	673
メーカー希望価格	mēkā kibō kakaku	manufacturer's suggested price, list price	673, 421, 643
希少	kishō	scarce, rare	144
希少価値	kishō kachi	scarcity value	144, 421, 425

677 ネ 5e

I, koromo – garment, clothes

衣類	irui	clothing	226
黒衣	kokui	black clothes	206
法衣	hōi	priestly robes, vestment	123
衣食住	ishokujū	food, clothing, and shelter	322, 156
羽衣	hagoromo	robe of feathers	590

678 亻 ネ 2a 5e

I, [E] – depend on, be due to; request

依存(度)	izon(do)	(extent of) dependence	269, 377
依然として	izen toshite	as ever, as before	651
帰依	kie	faith, devotion; conversion	317

679	ネ 刂 5e 2f	**SHO, haji(me)** – beginning; **haji(mete)** – for the first time; **hatsu-, ui-** – first; **-so(meru)** – begin to

最 初	saisho	beginning, first	263
初 歩	shoho	rudiments, ABCs	431
初 演	shoen	first performance, premiere	344
初 恋	hatsukoi	one's first love	258

初

680	糸 立 日 6a 5b 4c	**SHOKU, SHIKI, o(ru)** – weave

織 機	shokki	loom	528
組 織	soshiki	organization, structure; tissue	418
織 物	orimono	cloth, fabric, textiles	79
毛 織 (物)	keori(mono)	woolen fabric	287, 79
羽 織	haori	haori, Japanese half-coat	590

織

681	言 立 日 7a 5b 4c	**SHIKI** – know, discriminate

意 識	ishiki	consciousness	132
知 識	chishiki	knowledge	214
常 識	jōshiki	common sense/knowledge	497
学 識	gakushiki	learning	109
識 別	shikibetsu	discrimination, recognition	267

識

682	糸 戸 艹 6a 4m 3k	**HEN, a(mu)** – knit, crochet; compile, edit

編 集	henshū	editing	436
短 編 小 説	tanpen shōsetsu	short novel, story	215, 27, 400
編 成	hensei	organizing, formation	261
編 み 物	amimono	knitting; knitted goods	79
手 編 み	teami	knitting by hand	57

編

683	月 4b	口 2e	又 2h	**FUKU** – clothes, dress; dose			

衣服	ifuku	clothing	677
洋/和服	yō/wa-fuku	Western/Japanese clothing	289, 124
心服	shinpuku	admiration and devotion	97
着服	chakufuku	embezzlement, misappropriation	657
服役	fukueki	penal servitude; military service	375

684	土 (3b)	立 5b	十 2k	**KŌ, saiwa(i), shiawa(se), sachi** – happiness, good fortune			

幸運	kōun	good fortune, luck	439
不幸	fukō	unhappiness, misfortune	94

685	土 (3b)	立 5b	十 2k	**HŌ** – news, report; remuneration; **muku(iru)** – reward, requite			

天気予報	tenki yohō	weather forecast	141, 134, 393
報道機関	hōdō kikan	news media, the press	149, 528, 398
情報	jōhō	information	209
報知	hōchi	information, news, intelligence	214
電報	denpō	telegram	108

686	土 (3b)	立 5b	十 2k	**SHITSU, SHŪ, to(ru)** – take, grasp; carry out, execute			

執行	shikkō	execution, performance	68
執権	shikken	regent	335
執心	shūshin	devotion, attachment, infatuation	97
執着	shūjaku, shūchaku	attachment to; tenacity	657
執念	shūnen	tenacity of purpose; vindictiveness	579

687

火 口 亠
4d 3d 2j

JUKU, u(reru) – ripen, come to maturity

円熟	*enjuku*	maturity, mellowness	13
成熟	*seijuku*	ripeness, maturity	261
未熟	*mijuku*	unripe, immature, green	306
半熟	*hanjuku*	half-cooked, soft-boiled (egg)	88
熟語	*jukugo*	compound word; phrase	67

688

立 口 辛
5b 3b 2k2

JI – word; resignation; **ya(meru)** – quit, resign

辞書/典	*jisho/ten*	dictionary	131, 367
(お)世辞	*(o)seji*	compliment, flattery	252
式辞	*shikiji*	address, oration	525
辞職	*jishoku*	resignation	385
辞表	*jihyō*	(letter of) resignation	272

689

口 十 丨
3d 2k 1b

RAN – riot, rebellion; disorder; **mida(su/reru)** – put/get in disorder, confusion

反乱	*hanran*	rebellion, insurgency, insurrection	324
内乱	*nairan*	internal strife, civil war	84
乱雑	*ranzatsu*	disorder, confusion	575
乱筆	*ranpitsu*	hasty writing, scrawl	130

690

口 土 丿
3d 3b 1c

KOKU, tsu(geru) – tell, announce, inform

報告	*hōkoku*	report	685
通告	*tsūkoku*	notice, notification	150
申告	*shinkoku*	report, declaration, (tax) return	309
告発	*kokuhatsu*	prosecution, indictment, accusation	96
告白	*kokuhaku*	confession, avowal, profession	205

691	辶 土 口 2q 3b 3d	**ZŌ, tsuku(ru)** – produce, build

製造 　　　 seizō 　　　　 manufacture, production 　　　　　 428
造船 　　　 zōsen 　　　　　 shipbuilding 　　　　　　　　　 376
木造 　　　 mokuzō 　　　　 made of wood, wooden 　　　　　 22
人造 　　　 jinzō 　　　　　 man-made, artificial 　　　　　　 1
手造り 　　 tezukuri 　　　　 handmade 　　　　　　　　　　 57

692	氵 土 丷 3a 3b 2o	**SEN, ara(u)** – wash

洗剤 　　　　 senzai 　　　　 detergent 　　　　　　　　　　　 550
洗面器 　　　 senmenki 　　　 wash basin 　　　　　　　　 274, 527
洗面所 　　　 senmenjo 　　　 washroom, lavatory 　　　　　 274, 153
(お)手洗い 　 (o)tearai 　　　 washroom, lavatory 　　　　　　 57
洗い立てる 　 araitateru 　　　 inquire into, rake up, ferret out 　 121

693	氵 一 ノ 3a 1a2 1c	**O, kitana(i), kega(rawashii)** – dirty; **yogo(reru/su), kega(reru/su)** – become/make dirty

汚職 　　 oshoku 　　　 corruption, bribery 　　　　　　　　 385
汚物 　　 obutsu 　　　 dirt, filth; sewage 　　　　　　　　 79
汚点 　　 oten 　　　　 blot, blotch, blemish, tarnish 　　　 169
汚名 　　 omei 　　　　 stigma, stain on one's name, dishonor 　 82

694	广 ノ 丶 3q 1c 1d	**KŌ, hiro(i)** – broad, wide; **hiro(geru)** – extend, enlarge; **hiro(garu)** – spread, expand; **hiro(meru)** – broaden, propagate; **hiro(maru)** – spread, be propagated

広告 　　 kōkoku 　　　 advertisement 　　　　　　　　　 690
広大 　　 kōdai 　　　　 vast, extensive, huge 　　　　　　 26
広場 　　 hiroba 　　　　 plaza, public square 　　　　　　 154

695	糸 田 6a 5f	**SAI** – narrow, small, fine; **hoso(i)** – thin, narrow, slender; **hoso(ru)** – get thinner; **koma(kai/ka)** – small, detailed

委細	isai	details, particulars	466
細工	saiku	work, workmanship; artifice, trick	139
細説	saisetsu	detailed explanation	400
細長い	hosonagai	long and thin, lean and lanky	95

細

696	木 丶 ノ 4a 2o 1c	**SHŌ, matsu** – pine

松原	matsubara	pine grove	136
松林	matsubayashi	pine woods	127
松葉	matsuba	pine needle	253
門松	kadomatsu	pine decoration for New Year's	161
松島	Matsushima	(scenic coastal area near Sendai)	286

松

697	糸 心 丶 6a 4k 2o	**SŌ** – general, overall

総会	sōkai	general meeting, plenary session	158
総合	sōgō	synthesis, comprehensive	159
総計	sōkei	(sum) total	340
総理	sōri	prime minister (cf. No. 835)	143
国民総生産	kokumin sōseisan	gross national product	40, 177, 44, 278

総

698	宀 心 丶 3m 4k 2o	**SŌ, mado** – window

同窓生	dōsōsei	schoolmate, alumnus	198, 44
車窓	shasō	car window	133
窓口	madoguchi	(ticket) window	54
二重窓	nijūmado	double window	3, 227
窓際の席	madogiwa no seki	seat next to the window	618, 379

窓

699	氵 魚 3a 11a	**GYO, RYŌ** – fishing		
漁		漁業	gyogyō	fishery, fishing industry	279
		漁船	gyosen	fishing boat/vessel	376
		漁場	gyojō	fishing ground/banks	154
		漁村	gyoson	fishing village	191
		漁師	ryōshi	fisherman	409

700	魚 口 ⼨ 11a 3d 3n	**GEI, kujira** – whale		
鯨		白鯨	Hakugei	(Moby Dick, or The White Whale—Melville)	205
		鯨肉	geiniku	whale meat	223
		鯨油	geiyu	whale oil	364
		鯨飲	geiin	drink like a fish, guzzle	323

701	魚 王 ⼨ 11a 4f 2o	**SEN, aza(yaka)** – fresh, vivid, clear, brilliant		
鮮		新鮮	shinsen	fresh	174
		鮮明	senmei	clear, distinct	18
		鮮度	sendo	(degree of) freshness	377
		鮮魚	sengyo	fresh fish	290
		朝鮮	Chōsen	Korea	469

702	辶 王 尸 2q 4f 3r	**CHI, oso(i)** – late, tardy; slow; **oku(reru)** – be late (for); be slow (clock); **oku(rasu)** – defer, put back (a clock)		
遅		遅着	chichaku	late arrival	657
		遅配	chihai	delay in apportioning/delivery	515
		遅速	chisoku	speed	502
		乗り遅れる	noriokureru	be too late to catch, miss (a bus)	523

703 導

目 `` 辶
5c 2o 2q

DŌ, michibi(ku) – lead, guide

主 導	shudō	leadership, guidance	155
先 導	sendō	guidance, leadership	50
導 入	dōnyū	introduction	52
導 火 線	dōkasen	fuse; cause, occasion	20, 299
半 導 体	handōtai	semiconductor	88, 61

704 尊

`` 酉 十
2o 7e 2k

SON, tatto(bu), tōto(bu) – value, esteem, respect; **tatto(i), tōto(i)** – valuable, precious, noble, august

尊 重	sonchō	value, respect, pay high regard to	227
自 尊 (心)	jison(shin)	self-respect, pride	62, 97
尊 大	sondai	haughtiness, arrogance	26
本 尊	honzon	Buddha; idol; he himself, she herself	25

705 敬

夂 艹 口
4i 3k 3d

KEI, uyama(u) – respect, revere

尊 敬	sonkei	respect, deference	704
敬 意	keii	respect, homage	132
敬 老	keirō	respect for the aged	543
敬 遠	keien	keep at a respectful distance	446
敬 語	keigo	an honorific, term of respect	67

706 警

言 夂 艹
7a 4i 3k

KEI – admonish, warn

警 察	keisatsu	police	619
警 官	keikan	policeman	326
警 視	keishi	police superintendent	606
警 告	keikoku	warning, admonition	690
警 報	keihō	warning (signal), alarm	685

707	卩 土 一
	2e 3b 1a2

oro(su) – sell wholesale; ***oroshi*** – wholesaling

卸商	*oroshishō*	wholesaler	412
卸値	*oroshine*	wholesale price	425
卸し売り物価	*oroshiuri bukka*	wholesale prices	239, 79, 421

708	彳 土 卩
	3i 3b 2e

GYO, GO, on- – (honorific prefix)

制御	*seigyo*	control, governing, suppression	427
御飯	*gohan*	boiled rice; meal	325
御用の方	*goyō no kata*	customer, inquirer	107, 70
御所	*gosho*	imperial palace	153
御中	*onchū*	Dear sirs:, Gentlemen:, Messrs.	28

709	力 口
	2g 3d

KA, kuwa(eru) – add, append; ***kuwa(waru)*** – join, take part (in)

加入	*kanyū*	joining	52
加工	*kakō*	processing	139
加法	*kahō*	addition (in mathematics)	123
倍加	*baika*	doubling	87
付加価値税	*fukakachizei*	value-added tax	192, 421, 425, 399

710	彡 亻 一
	3j 2a 1a

SAN – three (in documents); go, come, visit; ***mai(ru)*** – go, come, visit, visit a temple/shrine

参加	*sanka*	participation	709
参列	*sanretsu*	attendance, presence	611
参議院	*Sangiin*	(Japanese) House of Councilors	292, 614
参考書	*sankōsho*	reference book/work	541, 131

711

一 艹 ノ
(1a) 3k 1c

弁

BEN – speech, dialect; discrimination; petal; valve

弁当	bentō	box/sack lunch	77
駅弁	ekiben	box lunch sold at a train station	284
答弁	tōben	reply, answer	160
弁解	benkai	explanation, justification, excuse	474
関西弁	Kansai-ben	Kansai dialect/accent	398, 72

712

土 田 日
3b 5f 4c

増

ZŌ, ma(su), fu(eru) – increase, rise; **fu(yasu)** – increase, raise

増加	zōka	increase, rise, growth	709
増産	zōsan	increase in production	278
増税	zōzei	tax increase	399
増進	zōshin	increase, furtherance, improvement	437

713

宀 田 口
3m 5f 3d

富

FU, [FŪ], tomi – wealth; **to(mu)** – be/become rich

国富	kokufu	national wealth	40
富強	fukyō	wealth and power	217
富力	furyoku	wealth, resources	100
富者	fusha, fūsha	rich person, the wealthy	164
富士山	Fuji-san	Mount Fuji	572, 34

714

刂 田 口
2f 5f 3d

副

FUKU – assistant, accompany, supplement

副社長	fukushachō	company vice-president	308, 95
副業	fukugyō	side business, sideline	279
副産物	fukusanbutsu	by-product	278, 79
副作用	fukusayō	side effects	360, 107
副題	fukudai	subtitle, subheading	354

715

氵 戈 口
3a 4n 3d

GEN, he(ru) – decrease, diminish; **he(rasu)** – decrease, shorten

増減	zōgen	increase and/or decrease	712
加減	kagen	addition and subtraction; state of health	709
減少	genshō	decrease, reduction	144
半減	hangen	reduction by half	88
減法	genpō	subtraction (in mathematics)	123

減

716

丷 皿 一
2o2 5h 1a

EKI, [YAKU] – profit, use, advantage

利益	rieki	profit, advantage	329
公益	kōeki	the public good	126
有益	yūeki	useful, beneficial, profitable	265
無益	mueki	useless, in vain	93
益鳥	ekichō	beneficial bird	285

益

717

皿 日 月
5h 4c 4b

MEI – oath; alliance

連盟	renmei	league, federation	440
同盟	dōmei	alliance, confederation	198
加盟	kamei	joining affiliation	709
盟主	meishu	the leader, leading power	155
盟約	meiyaku	pledge, pact; alliance	211

盟

718

言 戈 一
7a 4n 1a

SEI, makoto – truth, reality; sincerity, fidelity

誠実	seijitsu	sincere, faithful, truthful	203
誠意	seii	sincerity, good faith	132
誠心誠意	seishin-seii	sincerely, wholeheartedly	97, 132
誠に	makoto ni	truly, indeed; sincerely; very	

誠

719	皿 戈 一 5h 4n 1a	**SEI, [JŌ], saka(n)** – prosperous, energetic; **saka(ru)** – flourish, prosper; **mo(ru)** – serve (food); heap up

盛大	seidai	thriving, grand, magnificent	26
全盛	zensei	height of prosperity, zenith, heyday	89
最盛期	saiseiki	golden age, zenith	263, 449
花盛り	hanazakari	in full bloom, at its best	255

720	土 戈 一 3b 4n 1a	**JŌ, shiro** – castle

城下町	jōkamachi	castle town	31, 182
城主	jōshu	feudal lord of a castle	155
開城	kaijō	surrender of a fortress, capitulation	396
城門	jōmon	castle gate	161
古城	kojō	old castle	172

721	宀 口 ノ 3m 3d2 1c	**KYŪ, GŪ, [KU], miya** – shrine, palace, prince

宮城	kyūjō	imperial palace	720
神宮	jingū	Shinto shrine	310
宮参り	miyamairi	visit to a shrine	710
宮城県	Miyagi-ken	Miyagi Prefecture	720, 194
子宮	shikyū	uterus, womb	103

722	丷 口 冖 3n 3d2 2i	**EI, itona(mu)** – perform (a ceremony); conduct (business)

経営	keiei	management, administration	548
運営	un'ei	operation, management, running	439
公営	kōei	public management, municipally run	126
営業	eigyō	(running a) business	279
営利	eiri	profit, profit-making	329

723	〜 木 一 3n 4a 2i	**EI, ha(e)** – glory, honor, splendor; **ha(eru)** – shine, be brilliant; **saka(eru)** – thrive, prosper

栄養	eiyō	nutrition	402
光栄	kōei	honor, glory	138
栄光	eikō	glory	138
見栄え	mibae	outward appearance	63

724	〻 氵 一 (2b) 3a 1a	**KYŪ, moto(meru)** – want; request, demand, seek

請求	seikyū	a claim, demand	661
要求	yōkyū	demand	419
求職	kyūshoku	seeking employment, job hunting	385
求人	kyūjin	job offer, Help Wanted	1
探求	tankyū	research, investigation	535

725	攵 氵 一 4i 3a 1a	**KYŪ, suku(u)** – rescue, aid

救急	kyūkyū	first aid	303
救助	kyūjo	rescue, relief	623
救済	kyūsai	relief, aid, redemption, salvation	549
救命ボート	kyūmei bōto	lifeboat	578
救世軍	Kyūseigun	Salvation Army	252, 438

726	王 氵 一 4f 3a 1a	**KYŪ, tama** – ball, sphere

野球	yakyū	baseball	236
球場	kyūjō	baseball stadium, ball park	154
電球	denkyū	light bulb	108
(軽)気球	(kei)kikyū	(hot-air/helium) balloon	547, 134
地球	chikyū	the earth, globe	118

727	亻王戈 2a 4f 4n	**GI** – rule; ceremony; affair, matter

礼儀　　　　　*reigi*　　　　　politeness, courtesy, propriety　　　　　620
礼儀正しい　*reigi tadashii*　courteous, decorous　　　　　620, 275
儀式　　　　　*gishiki*　　　　ceremony, formality, ritual　　　　　525
儀典長　　　　*gitenchō*　　　chief of protocol　　　　　367, 95
地球儀　　　　*chikyūgi*　　　a globe　　　　　118, 726

728	牛王戈 4g 4f 4n	**GI** – sacrifice

729	牛土一 4g 3b 1a	**SEI** – sacrifice

犠牲　　　　*gisei*　　　　sacrifice　　　　　728
犠牲者　　　*giseisha*　　victim　　　　　728, 164

730	日土一 4c 3b 1a	**SEI, [SHŌ], hoshi** – star

火星　　　　*kasei*　　　　　Mars　　　　　20
明星　　　　*myōjō*　　　　　morning star, Venus　　　　　18
すい星　　　*suisei*　　　　comet
流れ星　　　*nagareboshi*　shooting star, meteor　　　　　247
星空　　　　*hoshizora*　　starry sky　　　　　140

731 牛 攵 4g 4i	**BOKU, maki** – pasture			
	牧場	*bokujō, makiba*	pasture, meadow	154
	牧草地	*bokusōchi*	pasture, grassland, meadowland	249, 118
	放牧	*hōboku*	pasturage, grazing	512
	牧羊者	*bokuyōsha*	sheep raiser, shepherd	288, 164
	牧師	*bokushi*	pastor, minister	409

732 亻 牛 2a 4g	**KEN** – matter, affair, case			
	事件	*jiken*	incident, affair, case	80
	条件	*jōken*	condition, terms, stipulation	564
	要件	*yōken*	important matter; condition, requisite	419
	用件	*yōken*	(item of) business	107
	案件	*anken*	matter, case, item	106

733 ⺈ 口 丷 2n 3s 2o	**MEN, manuka(reru)** – escape, avoid, be exempt from			
	御免	*gomen*	pardon; declining, refusal	708
	免責	*menseki*	exemption from responsibility	655
	免税	*menzei*	tax exemption	399
	免状	*menjō*	diploma; license	626
	免職	*menshoku*	dismissal from one's job/office	385

734 辶 口 ⺈ 2q 3s 2n	**ITSU** – idleness; diverge, deviate from			
	逸話	*itsuwa*	anecdote	238
	逸品	*ippin*	superb article, masterpiece	230
	放逸	*hōitsu*	self-indulgence, licentiousness	512

735	⺈ 口 力 2n 3s 2g	**BEN** – effort, hard work			
		勤勉	*kinben*	industriousness, diligence, hard work	559
		勉強	*benkyō*	studying; diligence; sell cheap	217
		勉強家	*benkyōka*	diligent student; hard worker	217, 165
		勉学	*bengaku*	study, pursuit of one's studies	109

勉

736	⽇ 口 ⺈ 4c 3s 2n	**BAN** – evening, night			
		今晩	*konban*	this evening, tonight	51
		毎晩	*maiban*	every evening	116
		一晩	*hitoban*	a night, all night	2
		朝晩	*asaban*	mornings and evenings, day and night	469
		晩年	*bannen*	latter part of one's life	45

晩

737	言 十 一 7a 2k 1a	**KYO, yuru(su)** – permit, allow			
		免許	*menkyo*	permission, license	733
		許可	*kyoka*	permission, approval, authorization	388
		許容	*kyoyō*	permission, tolerance	654
		特許	*tokkyo*	special permission; patent	282
		特許法	*tokkyohō*	patent law	282, 123

許

738	言 心 ⼑ 7a 4k 2f	**NIN, mito(meru)** – perceive; recognize; approve of			
		認可	*ninka*	approval	388
		認定	*nintei*	approval, acknowledgment	355
		確認	*kakunin*	confirmation, certification	603
		公認	*kōnin*	official recognition/sanction	126
		認識	*ninshiki*	cognition, recognition, perception	681

認

| 739 | ク 口 l | | | |
| | 2n 3s 1b | | | |

SHŌ – image, shape; **ZŌ** – elephant

具象的	gushōteki	concrete, embodied	420, 210
現象	genshō	phenomenon	298
対象	taishō	object, subject, target	365
気象学	kishōgaku	meteorology	134, 109
象げ	zōge	ivory	

象

| 740 | イ 口 ク | | | |
| | 2a 3s 2n | | | |

ZŌ – statue, image

仏像	butsuzō	statue/image of Buddha	583
自画像	jigazō	self-portrait	62, 343
受像機	juzōki	television set	260, 528
現像	genzō	(photographic) development	298
想像	sōzō	imagination	147

像

| 741 | 木 一 ノ | | | |
| | 4a2 1a 1c | | | |

kabu – share, stock; stump

株式会社	kabushiki-gaisha/kaisha	Co., Ltd.	525, 158, 308
株券	kabuken	share, stock certificate	506
株主	kabunushi	stockholder	155
株主総会	kabunushi sōkai	general meeting of shareholders	155, 697, 158
切り株	kirikabu	(tree) stump, (grain) stubble	39

株

| 742 | 糸 ク 一 | | | |
| | 6a 2n 1a2 | | | |

ZETSU, **ta(eru)** – die out, end; **ta(tsu)** – cut off, interrupt, eradicate; **ta(yasu)** – kill off, let die out

絶対	zettai	absolute	365
絶大	zetsudai	greatest, immense	26
絶望	zetsubō	despair	673
根絶	konzetsu	root out, eradicate, stamp out	314

絶

743	糸 木 日 6a 4a 4c	**REN, ne(ru)** – knead; train; polish up			

練習　　renshū　　practice, exercise　　　　　　　　　591
教練　　kyōren　　(military) drill　　　　　　　　　　245
試練　　shiren　　trial, test, ordeal　　　　　　　　　526
熟練　　jukuren　　practiced skill, expertness, mastery　687
洗練　　senren　　polish, refine　　　　　　　　　　692

744	日 イ 一 4c 2a2 1a4	**TAI, ka(eru)** – replace; **ka(waru)** – be replaced			

代替　　　　daitai　　　substitution　　　　　　　　　256
両替　　　　ryōgae　　　exchanging/changing money　　200
取り替え　　torikae　　　exchange, swap, replacement　　65
切り替え　　kirikae　　　renewal, changeover　　　　　39
着替える　　kigaeru, kikaeru　　change clothes　　　　657

745	貝 イ 一 7b 2a2 1a4	**SAN** – praise; agreement			

賛成　　sansei　　agreement, approbation　　　　　261
賛助　　sanjo　　support, backing　　　　　　　　623
協賛　　kyōsan　　approval, consent, support　　　234
賞賛　　shōsan　　praise, admiration　　　　　　　500
賛美　　sanbi　　praise, glorification　　　　　　401

746	士 厂 一 3p 2p 1a	**SEI, [SHŌ], koe, [kowa-]** – voice			

声明　　　　seimei　　　declaration, statement, proclamation　18
名声　　　　meisei　　　fame, renown, reputation　　　82
音声学　　　onseigaku　　phonetics　　　　　　　347, 109
声変わり　　koegawari　　change/cracking of voice　　257
声色　　　　kowairo　　　imitated/assumed voice　　　204

747 6f 5c 3k

SAN – calculate

計算	keisan	calculation, computation	340
公算	kōsan	probability, likelihood	126
予算	yosan	an estimate; budget	393
精算	seisan	exact calculation, (fare) adjustment	659
暗算	anzan	mental arithmetic/calculation	348

748 7b 4n 2a

TAI, ka(su) – rent out

貸与	taiyo	lend, loan	539
貸し家	kashiya	house for rent, rented house	165
貸しボート	kashibōto	boat for rent, rented boat	
貸し出す	kashidasu	lend/hire out	53
貸し切り	kashikiri	reservations, booking	39

749 7b 3h 1b2

HI, tsui(yasu) – spend; **tsui(eru)** – be wasted

経費	keihi	expenses, cost	548
費用	hiyō	expense, cost	107
生活費	seikatsuhi	living expenses, cost of living	44, 237
光熱費	kōnetsuhi	heating and lighting expenses	138, 645
旅費	ryohi	traveling expenses	222

750 7b 4j 2b

SHI – resources, capital, funds

資源	shigen	resources	580
資本	shihon	capital	25
資金	shikin	funds	23
物資	busshi	goods, (raw) materials	79
資格	shikaku	qualification, competence	643

297

---

751 貝 士 亻 (7b 3p 2a)

CHIN – rent, wages, fare, fee

賃金	chingin	wages, pay	23
賃上げ	chin'age	raise in wages	32
運賃	unchin	passenger fare; shipping charges	439
電車賃	denshachin	train fare	108, 133
家賃	yachin	rent	165

---

752 貝 亻 卜 (7b 2a 2m)

KA – freight; goods, property

貨物	kamotsu	freight	79
百貨店	hyakkaten	department store	14, 168
通貨	tsūka	currency	150
外貨	gaika	foreign goods/currency	83
銀貨	ginka	silver coin	313

---

753 貝 丷 刂 (7b 2o 2f)

HIN, BIN, mazu(shii) – poor

貧富	hinpu	poverty and wealth, the rich and poor	713
貧困	hinkon	poverty, need	558
貧弱	hinjaku	poor, meager, scanty	218
貧相	hinsō	poor-looking, seedy	146
清貧	seihin	honest poverty	660

---

754 一 丨 ノ (1a 1b 1c)

BŌ, tobo(shii) – scanty, meager, scarce

| 貧乏 | binbō | poor | 753 |
| 欠乏 | ketsubō | shortage, deficiency | 383 |

751 - 754

298

755 架 木 口 力 (4a 3d 2g)

KA, ka(keru) – hang, build (bridge); **ka(karu)** – hang, be built

架設	kasetsu	construction, laying	577
架橋	kakyō	bridge building	597
書架	shoka	bookshelf	131
十字架像	jūjikazō	crucifix	12, 110, 740
架空	kakū	overhead, aerial; fanciful	140

756 賀 貝 口 力 (7b 3d 2g)

GA – congratulations, felicitations

賀状	gajō	greeting card	626
年賀	nenga	New Year's greetings	45
年賀状	nengajō	New Year's card	45, 626
賀正	gashō	New Year's greetings	275
志賀高原	Shiga Kōgen	Shiga Highlands	573, 190, 136

757 収 又 丨 (2h 1b2)

SHŪ, osa(meru) – obtain, collect; **osa(maru)** – be obtained, end

収支	shūshi	income and expenditures	318
収入	shūnyū	income, earnings, receipts	52
買収	baishū	purchase; buying off, bribery	241
収益	shūeki	earnings, proceeds, profit	716
収容	shūyō	admission, accommodation	654

758 納 糸 冂 亻 (6a 2r 2a)

NŌ, [TŌ], [NA], [NA'], [NAN], osa(meru) – pay; supply; accept, store; **osa(maru)** – be paid (in), supplied

納税	nōzei	payment of taxes	399
出納	suitō	receipts and disbursements	53
納得	nattoku	consent, understanding	374
納屋	naya	(storage) shed	167

759	日 一 ノ 4c 1a 1c3	**EKI** – divination; **I, yasa(shii)** – easy						
		易者　　　ekisha　　　fortune-teller　　　　　　　　　　164 不易　　　fueki　　　immutability, unchangeableness　　94 交易　　　kōeki　　　trade, commerce, barter　　　　114 容易　　　yōi　　　easy, simple　　　　　　　　　　654 難易(度)　nan'i(do)　(degree of) difficulty　　557, 377							

760	貝 刂 厂 7b 2f 2p	**BŌ** – exchange, trade						
		貿易　　　　　bōeki　　　　trade　　　　　　　　　　　　759 自由貿易　　jiyū bōeki　　free trade　　　　　　62, 363, 759 貿易会社　　bōeki-gaisha　trading firm/company　759, 158, 308 貿易収支　　bōeki shūshi　balance of trade　　759, 757, 318 日米貿易　　Nichi-Bei bōeki　Japan-U.S. trade　　5, 224, 759							

761	田 刂 厂 5f 2f 2p	**RYŪ, [RU], to(meru)** – fasten down; hold, keep (in); **to(maru)** – stay, settle						
		留学　　　ryūgaku　　　study abroad　　　　　　　　109 留守　　　rusu　　　　absence from home　　　　　490 書留　　　kakitome　　registered mail　　　　　　131 局留(め)　kyokudome　general delivery　　　　　　170							

762	貝 宀 一 7b 3m 1a	**CHO** – storage						
		貯金　　　chokin　　　savings, deposit　　　　　　　23 貯水池　　chosuichi　reservoir　　　　　　　　21, 119							

763	广 一 丨
	3q 1a 1b

CHŌ – government office, agency

官庁	kanchō	government office, agency	326
警視庁	Keishichō	Metropolitan Police Department	706, 606
気象庁	Kishōchō	Meteorological Agency	134, 739
県庁	kenchō	prefectural office	194

庁

764	艹 日 一
	3k 4c 1a

SEKI, [SHAKU], mukashi – antiquity, long ago

今昔	konjaku	past and present	51
大昔	ōmukashi	remote antiquity, time immemorial	26
昔々	mukashimukashi	Once upon a time ...	
昔話	mukashibanashi	old tale, legend	238
昔の事	mukashi no koto	thing of the past	80

昔

765	心 日 艹
	4k 4c 3k

SEKI, o(shii) – regrettable; precious; wasteful; **o(shimu)** – regret; value; begrudge, be sparing of

惜敗	sekihai	narrow defeat (after a hard-fought contest)	511
愛惜	aiseki	be loath to part	259
口惜しい	kuchioshii	regrettable, vexing	54
負け惜しみ	makeoshimi	unwillingness to admit defeat	510

惜

766	亻 日 艹
	2a 4c 3k

SHAKU, ka(riru) – borrow, rent

借金	shakkin	debt	23
借財	shakuzai	debt	553
貸借	taishaku	debits and credits	748
転借	tenshaku	subleasing	433
賃借/借り	chin-shaku/gari	lease	751

借

767	夂月 艹 4i 4b 3k	*SAN, chi(rakasu)* – scatter, disarrange; *chi(rakaru)* – lie scattered, be in disorder; *chi(ru/rasu)* – (intr./tr.) scatter

解散	kaisan	breakup, dissolution, disbanding	474
散会	sankai	adjournment	158
散文	sanbun	prose	111
散歩	sanpo	walk, stroll	431

768	亻 艹 冂 2a 3k 2r	*BI, sona(eru)* – furnish, provide (for); *sona(waru)* – possess

設備	setsubi	equipment, facilities	577
整備	seibi	maintenance, servicing	503
軍備	gunbi	military preparations, armaments	438
予備費	yobihi	reserves, reserve funds	393, 749
備考	bikō	explanatory notes, remarks	541

769	頁 丨 9a 1b3	*JUN* – order, sequence

順番	junban	order, one's turn	185
順位	jun'i	ranking, standing	122
語順	gojun	word order	67
五十音順	gojū-on jun	in order of the kana syllabary	7, 12, 347
順調	junchō	favorable, smooth, without a hitch	342

770	广 一 丨 3q 1a2 1b	*JO* – beginning; preface; order, precedence

順序	junjo	order, method, procedure	769
序説	josetsu	introduction, preface	400
序論	joron	introduction, preface	293
序文	jobun	preface, foreword, introduction	111
序曲	jokyoku	overture, prelude	366

771	言丨 7a 1b3

訓

KUN – Japanese reading of a kanji; teaching, precept

訓育	kun'iku	education, discipline	246
教訓	kyōkun	teaching, precept, moral	245
訓練	kunren	training	743
訓辞	kunji	an admonitory speech, instructions	688
音訓	on-kun	Chinese and Japanese readings	347

772	目 厂 十 5c 2p 2k

盾

JUN, tate – shield

後ろ盾	ushirodate	support, backing, supporter, backer	48

773	一 丨 ノ 1a2 1b 1c

矛

MU, hoko – halberd

矛盾	mujun	contradiction	772
矛先	hokosaki	point of a spear; aim of an attack	50

774	木 一 丨 4a 1a2 1b

柔

JŪ, NYŪ, yawa(rakai/raka) – soft

柔道	jūdō	judo	149
柔術	jūjutsu	jujitsu	187
柔弱	nyūjaku	weakness, enervation	218
柔和	nyūwa	gentle, mild(-mannered)	124
物柔らか	monoyawaraka	mild(-mannered), quiet, gentle	79

775 辶 刂 (2q 2f)

辺

HEN, ata(ri), -be – vicinity

近辺	*kinpen*	neighborhood, vicinity	445
周辺	*shūhen*	periphery, environs	91
辺地	*henchi*	remote/out-of-the-way place	118
多辺地	*tahenchi*	polygon	229, 395
海辺	*umibe*	beach, seashore	117

776 辶 ノ 丶 (2q 1c 1d)

込

ko(mu) – be crowded, congested; **ko(meru)** – include, count in; load (a gun); concentrate

巻き込む	*makikomu*	entangle, involve, implicate	507
払い込む	*haraikomu*	pay in	582
申し込み	*mōshikomi*	proposal, offer, application	309
見込み	*mikomi*	prospects, outlook	63

777 辶 ノ (2q 1c3)

巡

JUN, megu(ru) – go around

巡回	*junkai*	tour, patrol, one's rounds	90
巡視	*junshi*	tour of inspection, round of visits	606
巡査	*junsa*	policeman, cop	624
巡礼	*junrei*	pilgrimage, pilgrim	620
巡業	*jungyō*	tour (of a troupe/team)	279

778 十 隹 氵 (2k 8c 3a)

準

JUN – semi-, quasi-; level; correspond (to)

水準	*suijun*	water level; level, standard	21
基準	*kijun*	standard, criterion	450
規準	*kijun*	criterion, standard, norm	607
準備	*junbi*	preparation	768
準決勝	*junkesshō*	semifinal game/round	356, 509

INDEX by Readings

(Kanji 1 – 778)

– D –

Reading	Kanji	No.
DAI	内	84
	代	256
	弟	405
	台	492
	大	26
	題	354
	第	404
DAN	団	491
	暖	635
	段	362
	男	101
	談	593
da(su)	出	53
DE	弟	405
DEN	伝	434
	田	35
	電	108
de(ru)	出	53
DO	土	24
	度	377
DŌ	働	232
	同	198
	動	231
	導	703
	堂	496
	童	410
	道	149
DOKU	毒	522
	独	219
	読	244
DON	曇	637

– E –

Reading	Kanji	No.
E	会	158
	依	678
	回	90
	絵	345
-e	重	227
EI	営	722
	映	352
	栄	723
	英	353
EKI	益	716
	役	375
	易	759
	液	472
	駅	284
EN	円	13
	園	447
	宴	640
	演	344
	遠	446
e(ru)	得	374

– F –

Reading	Kanji	No.
FU	不	94
	夫	315
	付	192
	婦	316
	富	713
	布	675
	府	504
	父	113
	符	505
	負	510
	風	29
	歩	431
	夫	315
	富	713
FŪ	風	29
fude	筆	130
fu(eru)	増	712
fuka(i)	深	536
fuka(maru)	深	536
fuka(meru)	深	536
fu(keru)	老	543
FUKU	副	714
	服	683
fumi	文	111
FUN	分	38
funa	船	376
fune	船	376
furu(i)	古	172
furu(su)	古	172
fuse(gu)	防	513
fushi	節	464
futa	二	3
futa(tsu)	二	3
futo(i)	太	629
futo(ru)	太	629
FUTSU	払	582
fu(yasu)	増	712
fuyu	冬	459

– G –

Reading	Kanji	No.
GA	画	343
	賀	756
GA'	合	159
GAI	外	83
	害	518
	街	186
GAKU	学	109
	楽	358
GAN	丸	644
	願	581
	元	137
	岸	586
	顔	277
GATSU	月	17
GE	下	31
	夏	461
	外	83
	解	474
GEI	芸	435
	鯨	700
GEN	元	137
	原	136
	減	715
	源	580
	現	298
	言	66
	験	532
GETSU	月	17
GI	儀	727
	犠	728
	義	291
	議	292
GIN	銀	313
GO	五	7
	午	49
	後	48
	御	708
	期	449
	語	67
	業	279
GŌ	合	159
	号	266
	強	217
GOKU	極	336
GON	勤	559
	権	335
	言	66
GU	具	420
GŪ	宮	721
GUN	軍	438
	郡	193
GYAKU	逆	444
GYO	御	708
	漁	699
	魚	290
GYŌ	業	279
	形	395
	行	68
GYOKU	玉	295
GYŪ	牛	281

– H –

Reading	Kanji	No.
HA	波	666
	破	665
HA'	法	123
ha	羽	590
	葉	253
	歯	478
habu(ku)	省	145
HACHI	八	10
ha(e)	栄	723
ha(eru)	映	352
	栄	723
haha	母	112
HAI	敗	511
	配	515
hai(ru)	入	52
haji(maru)	始	494
haji(me)	初	679
haji(meru)	始	494
haji(mete)	初	679
haka(rau)	計	340
haka(ru)	図	339
	量	411
	測	610
	計	340
hako(bu)	運	439
HAKU	博	601
	白	205
HAN	半	88
	反	324
	坂	443
	飯	325
hana	花	255
hana(reru)	放	512
hanashi	話	238
hana(su)	放	512
	話	238
hana(tsu)	放	512
hane	羽	590
hara	原	136
ha(rasu)	晴	662
hara(u)	払	582
ha(reru)	晴	662
hari	針	341
haru	春	460
hashi	橋	597
hashira	柱	598
hashi(ru)	走	429
hata	機	528
	畑	36
hatake	畑	36
hatara(ku)	働	232
ha(tasu)	果	487
ha(te)	果	487
ha(teru)	果	487
HATSU	発	96
hatsu-	初	679
haya(i)	早	248
	速	502
haya(maru)	早	248
haya(meru)	早	248
	速	502
hayashi	林	127
ha(yasu)	生	44
hazu(reru)	外	83
hazu(su)	外	83
HEI	平	202
	病	380
	閉	397
	陛	589
HEN	変	257
	編	682
	辺	775
	返	442
he(rasu)	減	715
he(ru)	減	715
	経	548
HI	費	749
	非	498
	飛	530
hi	日	5
	火	20
hidari	左	75
higashi	東	71
hikari	光	138
hika(ru)	光	138
hi(keru)	引	216
hi(ku)	引	216
hiku(i)	低	561
hiku(maru)	低	561
hiku(meru)	低	561
HIN	貧	753

	品 230		
hira	平 202		
hira(keru)	開 396		
hira(ku)	開 396		
hiro(garu)	広 694		
hiro(geru)	広 694		
hiro(i)	広 694		
hiro(maru)	広 694		
hiro(meru)	広 694		
hiru	昼 470		
hi(ru)	干 584		
hiruga(eru)	翻 596		
hirugae(su)	翻 596		
hito	人 1		
hito-	一 2		
hito(ri)	独 219		
hito(shii)	等 569		
hito(tsu)	一 2		
HITSU	必 520		
	筆 130		
hitsuji	羊 288		
HO	保 489		
	歩 431		
HO'	法 123		
ho	火 20		
HŌ	報 685		
	宝 296		
	方 70		
	放 512		
	法 123		
hodo	程 417		
hoka	外 83		
hoko	矛 773		
HOKU	北 73		
HON	本 25		
	反 324		
	翻 596		
hoshi	星 730		
hoso(i)	細 695		
hoso(ru)	細 695		
ho(su)	干 584		
hotoke	仏 583		
HOTSU	発 96		
HYAKU	百 14		
HYŌ	表 272		

– I –

I	以 46		
	位 122		
	依 678		
	医 220		
	易 759		
	委 466		
	衣 677		
	意 132		
ICHI	一 2		
ichi	市 181		
ie	家 165		
i(kasu)	生 44		
ike	池 119		
i(keru)	生 44		
ikio(i)	勢 646		
i(kiru)	生 44		

IKU	育 246	
i(ku)	行 68	
ikusa	戦 301	
ima	今 51	
imōto	妹 408	
IN	員 163	
	因 554	
	引 216	
	院 614	
	音 347	
	韻 349	
	飲 323	
inochi	命 578	
ino(ru)	祈 621	
inu	犬 280	
i(reru)	入 52	
iro	色 204	
i(ru)	入 52	
	居 171	
	要 419	
ishi	石 78	
iso(gu)	急 303	
ita(meru)	傷 633	
ita(mu)	傷 633	
ito	糸 242	
itona(mu)	営 722	
ITSU	一 2	
	逸 734	
itsu	五 7	
itsu(tsu)	五 7	
i(u)	言 66	

– J –

JAKU	弱 218	
	着 657	
	若 544	
JI	事 80	
	仕 333	
	侍 571	
	次 384	
	寺 41	
	地 118	
	字 110	
	持 451	
	時 42	
	治 493	
	示 615	
	耳 56	
	自 62	
	辞 688	
JI'	十 12	
-ji	路 151	
JIKI	直 423	
	食 322	
JIN	人 1	
	神 310	
JITSU	実 203	
	日 5	
JO	助 623	
	女 102	
	序 770	
JŌ	乗 523	
	上 32	

	城 720	
	場 154	
	条 564	
	定 355	
	常 497	
	情 209	
	成 261	
	浄 664	
	状 626	
	盛 719	
	静 663	
	授 602	
	受 260	
JŪ	重 227	
	住 156	
	十 12	
	柔 774	
JUKU	熟 687	
JUN	盾 772	
	旬 338	
	準 778	
	順 769	
	巡 777	
JUTSU	術 187	

– K –

KA	下 31	
	可 388	
	夏 461	
	果 487	
	化 254	
	何 390	
	価 421	
	加 709	
	家 165	
	架 755	
	歌 392	
	河 389	
	火 20	
	科 255	
	花 391	
	荷 488	
	課 752	
	過 413	
KA'	合 159	
-ka	日 5	
kabu	株 741	
kado	角 473	
	門 161	
kaeri(miru)	省 145	
kae(ru)	帰 317	
	返 442	
ka(eru)	変 257	
	代 256	
	替 744	
kae(su)	帰 317	
	返 442	
KAI	介 453	
	会 158	
	回 90	
	改 514	
	街 186	

	械 529	
	皆 587	
	海 117	
	界 454	
	絵 345	
	解 474	
	開 396	
	階 588	
kai	貝 240	
ka(karu)	架 755	
ka(keru)	架 755	
	欠 383	
KAKU	画 343	
	各 642	
	客 641	
	格 643	
	確 603	
	覚 605	
	角 473	
ka(ku)	欠 383	
	書 131	
kami	上 32	
	神 310	
	紙 180	
	完 613	
	官 326	
KAN	寒 457	
	巻 507	
	干 584	
	刊 585	
	感 262	
	漢 556	
	管 328	
	観 604	
	間 43	
	関 398	
	館 327	
kan	神 310	
kana	金 23	
kanara(zu)	必 520	
kane	金 23	
kanga(eru)	考 541	
kao	顔 277	
kara	空 140	
karada	体 61	
ka(riru)	借 766	
karo(yaka)	軽 547	
karu(i)	軽 547	
kasa(naru)	重 227	
kasa(neru)	重 227	
kashira	頭 276	
ka(su)	貸 748	
kata	形 395	
	方 70	
katachi	形 395	
kata(i)	難 557	
kataki	敵 416	
katana	刀 37	
kata(rau)	語 67	
kata(ru)	語 67	
KATSU	割 519	
	活 237	
ka(tsu)	勝 509	
ka(u)	交 114	

Reading	Kanji	No.
mamo(ru)	守	490
MAN	万	16
	満	201
mana(bu)	学	109
mane(ku)	招	455
manuka(reru)	免	733
maru	丸	644
maru(i)	丸	644
	円	13
maru(meru)	丸	644
masa(ni)	正	275
masa(ru)	勝	509
ma(su)	増	712
mato	的	210
MATSU	末	305
matsu	松	696
ma(tsu)	待	452
matsu(ri)	祭	617
matsurigoto	政	483
matsu(ru)	祭	617
matta(ku)	全	89
mawa(ri)	周	91
mawa(ru)	回	90
mawa(su)	回	90
ma(zaru)	交	114
ma(zeru)	交	114
mazu(shii)	貧	753
me	目	55
	女	102
megu(ru)	巡	777
MEI	命	578
	名	82
	明	18
	盟	717
MEN	免	733
	面	274
meshi	飯	325
MI	未	306
	味	307
mi	三	4
	実	203
	身	59
michi	道	149
michibi(ku)	導	703
mi(chiru)	満	201
mida(reru)	乱	689
mida(su)	乱	689
midori	緑	537
mi(eru)	見	63
migi	右	76
mijika(i)	短	215
mimi	耳	56
MIN	民	177
mina	皆	587
minami	南	74
minamoto	源	580
minato	港	669
mino(ru)	実	203
mi(ru)	見	63
mise	店	168
mi(seru)	見	63
mi(tasu)	満	201
mito(meru)	認	738
mi(tsu)	三	4
mit(tsu)	三	4
miya	宮	721
miyako	都	188
mizu	水	21
mizuka(ra)	自	62
mizuumi	湖	467
MŌ	亡	672
	毛	287
	望	673
mochi(iru)	用	107
mo(eru)	燃	652
mō(keru)	設	577
MOKU	木	22
	目	55
MON	文	111
	門	161
	問	162
	聞	64
mono	物	79
	者	164
moppa(ra)	専	600
mori	守	490
	森	128
mo(ru)	盛	719
mo(shikuwa)	若	544
mo(su)	燃	652
mō(su)	申	309
moto	下	31
	本	25
	元	137
	基	450
motoi	基	450
moto(meru)	求	724
MOTSU	物	79
mo(tsu)	持	451
motto(mo)	最	263
mo(yasu)	燃	652
MU	無	93
	矛	773
	務	235
mu	六	8
mugi	麦	270
mui	六	8
mukashi	昔	764
mu(kau)	向	199
mu(keru)	向	199
mu(kō)	向	199
mu(ku)	向	199
muku(iru)	報	685
mura	村	191
muro	室	166
musu(bu)	結	485
mu(tsu)	六	8
mut(tsu)	六	8
muzuka(shii)	難	557
MYŌ	命	578
	名	82
	明	18

– N –

Reading	Kanji	No.
NA	南	74
	納	758
NA'	納	758
na	名	82
naga(i)	長	95
naga(reru)	流	247
naga(su)	流	247
nago(mu)	和	124
nago(yaka)	和	124
NAI	内	84
na(i)	亡	672
	無	93
naka	中	28
naka(ba)	半	88
nama	生	44
nami	波	666
NAN	南	74
	男	101
	納	758
	難	557
nan	何	390
nana	七	9
nana(tsu)	七	9
nani	何	390
nano	七	9
nao(ru)	直	423
	治	493
nao(su)	直	423
	治	493
nara(u)	習	591
na(ru)	成	261
nasa(ke)	情	209
na(su)	成	261
natsu	夏	461
ne	値	425
	根	314
	音	347
nega(u)	願	581
NEN	年	45
	念	579
	然	651
	燃	652
ne(ru)	練	743
NETSU	熱	645
NI	二	3
ni	荷	391
NICHI	日	5
niga(i)	苦	545
niga(ru)	苦	545
nii-	新	174
NIKU	肉	223
NIN	人	1
	任	334
	認	738
nishi	西	72
no	野	236
NŌ	能	386
	納	758
	農	369
nobo(ru)	上	32
nobo(seru)	上	32
nobo(su)	上	32
nochi	後	48
noko(ru)	残	650
noko(su)	残	650
no(mu)	飲	323
no(ru)	乗	523
no(seru)	乗	523
nozo(mu)	望	673
nuno	布	675
nushi	主	155
NYAKU	若	544
NYO	女	102
NYŌ	女	102
NYŪ	入	52
	柔	774

– O –

Reading	Kanji	No.
O	悪	304
	汚	693
	和	124
o-	小	27
ō-	央	351
	奥	476
	王	294
	皇	297
	大	26
obo(eru)	覚	605
o(eru)	終	458
ō(i)	多	229
ō(ini)	大	26
ō(iru)	老	543
ō(kii)	大	26
o(kiru)	起	373
okona(u)	行	68
oko(ru)	興	368
	起	373
oko(su)	興	368
	起	373
OKU	億	382
	屋	167
	憶	381
	奥	476
oku	置	426
oku(rasu)	遅	702
oku(reru)	後	48
	遅	702
oku(ru)	送	441
omo	主	155
	面	274
omo(i)	重	227
omote	表	272
	面	274
omo(u)	思	99
ON	恩	555
	温	634
	遠	446
	音	347
on-	御	708
ona(ji)	同	198
onna	女	102
onoono	各	642
onore	己	370
o(riru)	下	31
oroshi	卸	707
oro(su)	卸	707
o(rosu)	下	31
o(ru)	織	680
osa(maru)	収	757
	治	493

Reading	Kanji	No.
	城	720
shiro(i)	白	205
shi(ru)	白	205
shiru(su)	知	214
	記	371
shita	下	31
shita(shii)	親	175
shita(shimu)	親	175
SHITSU	失	311
	執	686
	室	166
	質	176
shizu	静	663
shizu(ka)	静	663
shizu(maru)	静	663
shizu(meru)	静	663
SHO	所	153
	暑	638
	書	131
	初	679
SHŌ	正	275
	少	144
	省	145
	商	412
	傷	633
	上	32
	声	746
	小	27
	掌	499
	賞	500
	性	98
	招	455
	政	483
	星	730
	松	696
	相	146
	渉	432
	清	660
	将	627
	生	44
	精	659
	紹	456
	勝	509
	証	484
	象	739
	青	208
SHOKU	植	424
	織	680
	職	385
	色	204
	食	322
SHU	主	155
	守	490
	手	57
	酒	517
	種	228
	取	65
	首	148
SHŪ	州	195
	周	91
	収	757
	執	686
	宗	616
	秋	462
	終	458
	習	591
	週	92
	集	436
SHUKU	宿	179
SHUN	春	460
SHUTSU	出	53
SO	想	147
	祖	622
	素	271
	組	418
SŌ	争	302
	宗	616
	想	147
	早	248
	相	146
	窓	698
	総	697
	草	249
	走	429
	送	441
soda(teru)	育	246
soda(tsu)	育	246
soko	底	562
soko(nau)	損	350
soko(neru)	損	350
SOKU	束	501
	側	609
	測	610
	即	463
	則	608
	足	58
	速	502
-so(meru)	初	679
SON	尊	704
	存	269
	損	350
	村	191
sona(eru)	供	197
	備	768
sona(waru)	備	768
sono	園	447
sora	空	140
so(rasu)	反	324
so(ru)	反	324
soso(gu)	注	357
soto	外	83
SU	主	155
	子	103
	守	490
	数	225
	素	271
	州	195
SŪ	数	225
sue	末	305
su(giru)	過	413
su(gosu)	過	413
SUI	出	53
	水	21
su(i)	酸	516
suke	助	623
suko(shi)	少	144
su(ku)	好	104
suku(nai)	少	144
suku(u)	救	725
su(masu)	済	549
su(mau)	住	156
sumi(yaka)	速	502
su(mu)	住	156
	済	549
susu(meru)	進	437
susu(mu)	進	437

– T –

Reading	Kanji	No.
TA	他	120
	多	229
	太	629
ta	手	57
	田	35
taba	束	501
ta(beru)	食	322
tabi	度	377
	旅	222
tada(chini)	直	423
tada(shii)	正	275
tada(su)	正	275
ta(eru)	絶	742
TAI	代	256
	体	61
	台	492
	大	26
	太	629
	待	452
	態	387
	対	365
	替	744
	貸	748
tai(ra)	平	202
taka	高	190
taka(i)	高	190
taka(maru)	高	190
taka(meru)	高	190
takara	宝	296
take	竹	129
TAKU	宅	178
	度	377
tama	玉	295
	球	726
tame(su)	試	526
tami	民	177
tamo(tsu)	保	489
TAN	単	300
	探	535
	短	215
	反	324
tane	種	228
tani	谷	653
tano(shii)	楽	358
tano(shimu)	楽	358
ta(riru)	足	58
ta(ru)	足	58
tashi(ka)	確	603
tashi(kameru)	確	603
ta(su)	足	58
tasu(karu)	助	623
tasu(keru)	助	623
tataka(u)	戦	301
tate	盾	772
ta(teru)	立	121
tato(eru)	例	612
TATSU	達	448
ta(tsu)	立	121
	絶	742
tatto(bu)	尊	704
tatto(i)	尊	704
ta(yasu)	絶	742
tayo(ri)	便	330
te	手	57
TEI	丁	184
	体	61
	低	561
	弟	405
	定	355
	底	562
	抵	560
	提	628
	程	417
	邸	563
TEKI	敵	416
	的	210
	適	415
TEN	天	141
	典	367
	点	169
	店	168
	転	433
tera	寺	41
TETSU	鉄	312
TO	図	339
	土	24
	度	377
	徒	430
	渡	378
	頭	276
	都	188
to	十	12
	戸	152
TŌ	東	71
	島	286
	刀	37
	冬	459
	当	77
	党	495
	湯	632
	答	160
	等	569
	納	758
	読	244
	頭	276
	道	149
tō	十	12
to(basu)	飛	530
tobo(shii)	乏	754
to(bu)	飛	530
to(i)	問	162
tō(i)	遠	446
to(jiru)	閉	397
to(kasu)	解	474
to(keru)	解	474
toki	時	42
toko-	常	497